Critical Guides to French Texts

66 Sartre: Les Mots

Critical Guides to French Texts

EDITED BY ROGER LITTLE, WOLFGANG VAN EMDEN, DAVID WILLIAMS

SARTRE

Les Mots

Denis Boak

Professor of French Studies
University of Western Australia

Grant & Cutler Ltd
1987

© Grant & Cutler Ltd
1987

Library of Congress Cataloging-in-Publication Data

Boak, Denis.
 Sartre.Les mots.

 (Critical guides to French texts: 66)
 Bibliography: p.
 1. Sartre, Jean Paul, 1905-1980. Mots. 2. Sartre, Jean Paul, 1905-1980
—Biography. 3. Authors, French—20th century—Biography—History and
criticism. 4. Philosophers—France—Biography—History and criticism. 5.
Autobiography. I. Title.
PQ2637.A82Z575 1987 848'.91409 [B] 87-23674
ISBN 0-7293-0273-3

I.S.B.N. 84-599-2169-7

DEPÓSITO LEGAL: V. 2.582 - 1987

Printed in Spain by
Artes Gráficas Soler, S.A., Valencia
for
GRANT & CUTLER LTD
55-57, GREAT MARLBOROUGH STREET, LONDON W1V 2AY
and
27, SOUTH MAIN STREET, WOLFEBORO, NH 03894-2069, USA

Contents

Preface

Sartre, in his prime, accused critics of being no more than 'gardiens de cimetière', which has not stopped his work attracting as much critical attention as that of any writer of the age. Too much, some might claim; but any diffidence one might feel at adding to this mountain has to be tempered with the knowledge that Sartre himself spent much of his last three decades of active life on work which can only be described, in the broad sense, as criticism. And since *Les Mots* is by common acclaim one of the most brilliant books of the century, this alone would justify a critical monograph in English.

My method is, I hope, straightforward. I open with some general reflections on autobiography as a literary genre, then examine the form of *Les Mots* in their light. The bulk of my study is a detailed analysis of the text, followed by general comments on the work, its form and content, and finally a subjective appreciation of its value and place in the French literary tradition.

Quotations from *Les Mots* are followed by the page number in the most accessible edition, the Folio paperback (1972). The pagination of this runs from 11 to 214; readers using the Methuen's Twentieth Century Texts edition by David Nott (1981), with closely similar pagination from 3 to 213, should rapidly be able to calibrate. Italicized numbers in brackets refer to the numbered items in the Select Bibliography at the end of this volume.

For convenience, I shall throughout call the boy Sartre 'Poulou', keeping 'Sartre' for the mature man and writer. Again, I shall usually simply use the name 'Karl' for Sartre's grandfather Karl/Charles Schweitzer, 'Louise' for his grandmother, Karl's wife Louise Guillemin, and 'Anne-Marie' for his mother Anne-Marie Sartre, later Mancy.

Chronological Summary

1844	Birth of Charles (Karl) Schweitzer (d.1935), m. Louise Guillemin (1849-1930).
1882	Birth of Anne-Marie Schweitzer.
1904	Marriage of Anne-Marie to Jean-Baptiste Sartre (b.1874).
1905	June 21, birth of Jean-Paul Sartre (Poulou).
1906	Death of Jean-Baptiste Sartre.
1906-11	Anne-Marie and Poulou live with Karl and Louise at Meudon, outside Paris.
1909	Karl retires from his post as *professeur de lycée*.
1911-17	Karl, Louise, Anne-Marie and Poulou move to Rue Le Goff, Paris V^e.
1917	Anne-Marie marries Joseph Mancy.
1917-20	Poulou, mother and stepfather live at La Rochelle.
1920-22	Sartre's *baccalauréat* years, at Lycée Henri IV.
1922-24	*Khâgne*, preparation for Ecole Normale Supérieure, Lycée Louis Le Grand.
1924-28	Ecole Normale Supérieure.
1929	*Agrégation de philosophie*, after failing humiliatingly in 1928; meets Simone de Beauvoir.
1929-31	Military service, in army meteorological branch.
1931-33	Teaches philosophy, Lycée du Havre.
1933-34	Scholarship at French Institute, Berlin.
1934-39	Teaches philosophy, Le Havre and Laon.
1938	*La Nausée*.
1939	*Le Mur*.
1939	Called back to the army.
1940	Prisoner-of-war.
1941	Released from captivity in Germany.
1943	*L'Etre et le néant*.
1944	Liberation of France; Sartre internationally famous and henceforth rarely out of the public eye.

1945	Death of Joseph Mancy; Sartre lives with Anne-Marie from 1946 to 1962.
1945-49	*Les Chemins de la liberté.*
1960	*Critique de la raison dialectique.*
1963	October-November, publication of *Les Mots* in *Les Temps modernes.*
1964	January, *Les Mots* appears in book form.
1969	Death of Anne-Marie Mancy.
1971-72	*L'Idiot de la famille.*
1973	Virtually blind.
1980	April 15, death of Sartre.

1. Introduction

Ever since St Augustine, autobiography has formed a unique strand of Western literary culture, one which runs through Cellini, Rousseau, and Goethe, to the immense popularity of the genre today. Yet only recently has it become the focus of informed critical attention. What immediately emerges from this analysis is that it is by no means as straightforward a literary form as might first appear. Autobiography is a highly complex genre, supremely problematical, fraught with uncertainty, ambiguities, and equivocation; perhaps even more so than the novel, since in fiction the question of historical truth does not apply. What does is plausibility, a very different matter.

The only really unassailable definition of autobiography is one so bland and simple as to seem of little use: something like 'a person's account of his or her own life'. Any attempt to make the definition more detailed will prove to introduce unacceptable restrictions and make it prescriptive rather than descriptive and inclusive. An account in prose? Usually, but not necessarily; a verse autobiography is perfectly possible, such as Wordsworth's *Prelude*. Written in the first person? Again, not always: Caesar's war memoirs are written in the third person, and one could even conceive of a second-person autobiography, following the fictional precedent of Michel Butor's *La Modification*. (It has indeed recently been done, very creditably, in Alain Bosquet's *L'Enfant que tu étais* [1982].) And any other formal limitation can be seen as arbitrary and unjustifiable.

It is when we come to examine the motives for writing autobiography that we are forced to acknowledge exactly how slippery and ambivalent they are. At first sight, it seems a reasonable enough aim to wish to chronicle for posterity the uniqueness of a human existence; yet some, like Dostoevsky, have excoriated this as an intolerable and shameful manifestation of human egoism and vanity. On this view, every human life is *sub specie aeternitatis* unique and equally valuable, and it is therefore monstrous to declare one's own life so qualitatively superior to the general run as to be of interest to others. In reality, this argument seems to me refuted by the very popularity of the genre. Even if it is a subjective judgment to deem one's life worthy of record, that judgment is ratified if the autobiography strikes a chord among a readership. And ever since the Romantics, introspection and obsession with the self have been artistically respectable to the highest degree.

The idea of recording the uniqueness of one's existence implies, however, total respect for truth, yet motives for autobiography may cover very different attitudes. We need only think of the memoirs of the great, or would-be great, politicians and generals in particular, to see that truth weighs very lightly in attempts to erect a monument for posterity, except as an obstacle in the shape of inconvenient facts. The whole idea of self-questioning may be rejected as intolerable weakness. Autobiography may be intended to conceal the truth as well as reveal it; even an apparently confessional work may not be factually reliable. Did Rousseau, or did he not, abandon his illegitimate children to a foundling hospital?

There are indeed many different motives, or combinations of motives, rational or emotional, conscious or unconscious, for attempting autobiography, mostly it is true closely tied to the ego of the writer, if not therefore necessarily discreditable. If modesty is not among them, this still leaves a long list. Nostalgia, self-justification, publicity, preaching, family piety, confession, exhibitionism, self-glorification, complaint, revenge, setting the world to rights, autocatharsis or therapy, exorcism of humiliation, compensation, celebration of times past, or desire to relive or escape into them, hope to be remembered after one's death, testimony to unusual events one has happened to witness, or a way of life, or places in time, an attempt to understand society, the age, or the nature of human existence, or oneself, even simply the garrulous tendency to reminisce in advancing age — the catalogue could be extended, not forgetting compulsive lying. Usually too there will be the desire to do the job successfully, both on the mundane level of selling the book and making money, and the more aspiring one of hoping for literary fame, which explains the employment of ghosts by the less articulate. For literary professionals, we may add a desire to emulate, even to excel, existing classics in the genre, perhaps also to demonstrate consummate ability in handling language; or, given the premium on originality which has dominated all Western art since the Romantics, a wish to do the thing differently as well as better.

Disentangling this skein of motivation can be far from simple, especially since concealment may be as important as revelation. In Sartre's case, many of these elements come into play, some as part of a deliberate 'project', others possibly without his full consciousness. Moreover, a major breakthrough in understanding Sartre has been the realization that, usually, he was quite literally writing about himself. Not only in the fiction and drama, but also in the biographical studies, and even in the philosophy. Sartre's Existentialism is not so much a form of solipsism or extreme subjectivism, but of narcissism, obsession with self; and this takes the form of self-hatred as well as self-love, together with a pathological thirst to attack others as a means of self-defence.

Professional writers naturally have a head start, simply by knowing how to handle a pen, and it is no surprise that so many renowned autobiographies have been composed by writers with an established literary reputation. There is indeed a special attraction in the genre for the novelist, whose stock-in-trade is material from which to weave fictions, with the constant danger of exhausting this and therefore inspiration. Such a writer can always, *faute de mieux*, turn to his own life. But without needing to assume that a decline in creative imagination is the motive, it is perhaps more common than not for well-known writers to turn to autobiography, or if not, for critics to start wondering why. Moreover, the professional may have a more noble motive, seeing autobiography as the 'ouvrage suprême, celui qui englobe, explique et justifie tout ce qui précède',[1] or what one might, in the fashionable jargon, label a 'metatext'.

---

[1] G. May, *L'Autobiographie*, P.U.F., 1979, p.33. Professor May's book seems to me the best general introduction to the genre, combining a sensible down-to-earth approach with considerable erudition.

Somerset Maugham, it is true, claimed that no novelist can write a good autobiography, since all worthwhile experience will have gone, however disguised, into the novels; but the very autobiographies by novelists accepted as classics, including Maugham's own *The Summing Up*, prove this claim plainly untenable — or false modesty. Christopher Isherwood, on the other hand, asserted that 'good autobiography is only achieved when its live original has qualities which would make him a suitable hero for a novel'. This begs the question, because some might say that anyone at all, however ordinary, can be a novel-hero, the skill being all in the writing. Be that as it may, the vast majority of autobiographies have indeed been produced by individuals who have already made their mark, rather than by humble ordinary folk; and even where an author claims to be unexceptional, this may be no more than the rhetoric of modesty. All else apart, there is the overriding problem of persuading publishers to accept a work by an unknown; the famous are virtually guaranteed publication, even if they have done no more than lend their name to a ghost. It might even be maintained that the very fact of being able to communicate a life effectively to readers takes the writer out of the category of the ordinary, though this argument is probably circular. In the end it is likely that the successful autobiography will contain a combination of familiar and unfamiliar elements of human experiences (as will indeed the successful novel): not so unfamiliar as to make the reader feel completely alienated, nor so familiar as to offer nothing new.

The professional will also be able to avoid other pitfalls for the novice autobiographer, such as the assumption that recollections of people, or events, unforgettably important or deliciously nostalgic to the author, become equally so to the reader by the very fact of being introduced in the narrative. But this very question of literary ability raises other problems: how can it be reconciled with the demands of historical truth? A naïve view would require the style of autobiographical narrative to be plain and unadorned, since stylistic polish would detract from the 'transparency' of the account, its immediacy and therefore its authenticity. Yet this view cannot be sustained: what appears to the reader as 'sincerity', 'transparency', plain-speaking, is usually itself the product of literary skill, not of aesthetic innocence. This is not to say that it is not, arguably, superior as a form of autobiographical communication to a highly self-conscious or convoluted style; but, in art, another word for innocence is ignorance, and the real product of the unpractised pen is less likely to be directness and immediacy than clumsiness. In any case, the very act of putting memories into words to some extent deforms them, just as one cannot behave entirely naturally when looking at oneself in a mirror.

A certain amount of distortion is thus inevitable, even with the best will in the world. Often this is lacking, and the distortion is deliberate, as in the various forms of image-polishing: the author attributing to himself a role more interesting or admirable than he knows to be the case, or, on the negative side but no less importantly, omitting or concealing facts or memories which do not redound to his credit. Indeed, what is omitted may be just as significant as what is included, in a rounded picture of the author, but without access to other sources of information, this will never be known. The latitude for straightforward falsifying of the record is considerable. Some omissions may be more creditable, such as the desire not to hurt or embarrass friends or persons still living, or — a powerful motive often underrated — the fear of libel actions. But the result is the same as far as historical accuracy is concerned: the full picture is not communicated. In any case, of course, it is necessary for the author to make a choice among memories, however faithfully preserved: total recall does not make for digestible reading any more than for easy listening. This choice will be to a large extent aesthetically, not historically, motivated.

At an unconscious, or pre-conscious, level come all the distortions caused by imperfect memory. These may to some extent be corrected if the autobiographer has documented sources available, such as diaries or letters, less likely when dealing with childhood than later years. Most autobiographies are not written until the maturity of the author, by which time childhood memories are far from fresh. These will have become petrified, memories of memories, even memories of memories of memories, probably tinged with or transformed by such emotions as nostalgia or a sense of humiliation. Of course it can be maintained that all memories must be of psychological importance, whatever their degree of historical accuracy, since otherwise they would not have been retained; yet this argument too is clearly circular, and it must remain debatable whether all early memories are in fact purposeful, or some at least simply arbitrary and fragmentary. It is true, though, that what matters to the writer is not so much the actual experience, by this time hopelessly lost in the past, as the content of the memory, whether deformed or not. In the end, no autobiography is going to be completely reliable as a historical record, though there are different degrees of distortion, with different motives. To this extent we may agree with Georges May that the problem of truth in autobiography is a 'faux problème'.

Another consideration, highly relevant in Sartre's case, is that any attempt to discover a meaningful pattern or design in memories is artificial, an unjustifiable imposition after the fact, since in the actual chaotic day-to-day living of our lives no such pattern exists, and the significance of events often completely escapes us until later, possibly much later. It is indeed a professional deformation of historians to find a closed and inevitable pattern in events which once belonged to a problematic and open future: as Kierkegaard put it, 'life is lived forwards but can only be explained backwards'. Ironically, this is the main reason why Roquentin abandons his biography of Rollebon in *La Nausée*, once he comes to the conclusion that it is an artificial distortion to attempt to force on lived events any kind of order inseparable from a consistent narrative. Meaning, on this argument, is always an unjustified superimposition on life itself. The difference is that Roquentin, working on historical documents in the Bouville public library, is presumably trying to get to the truth of the matter, while Sartre in *Les Mots* is more interested in *creating* a meaning.

Such considerations have led critics to question the idea of any clear demarcation between autobiography and the novel, since in the one genre all novels are likely to contain autobiographical elements, and in the other, various distortions will detract from absolute historical accuracy. An extreme position would deny any distinction at all between the two. This is perhaps excessive: it is difficult to deny that autobiography must stand in *some* relationship to actual events which have happened to the narrator, or which are at least claimed to. On this basis, we are probably left with a definition of autobiography including any work which purports to be one and cannot be demonstrated to be purely fictional.

What is evident is that the relationship between auto-biography and novel is nowhere near as clear-cut as was once thought. Autobiography, and indeed biography, can certainly be read in the same frame of mind, or of appreciation, as fiction, with imaginative plausibility the ultimate criterion, rather than a possibly unattainable historical accuracy. Yet most of us probably do read what is known to Anglo-Saxons as non-fiction (a category unknown to French libraries) in a different way from novels; rightly or wrongly, we are in some way reassured by its supposed basis in fact, and disappointed or annoyed where apparent fact is demonstrably false. Yet although the criterion of plausibility is considerably narrower in the novel than in ordinary life, where we simply have to accept improbabilities, inconsistencies or wild coincidences which would offend us in fiction, the autobiographer is still faced with the problem of convincing the reader and of making his apparently factual world acceptable, though the criterion is interpreted more broadly. Something of the same sort of problem exists at other frontiers of the novel: in recent years the 'roman-reportage' has come to be taken much more seriously than before, and in it there are many parallels with the relation-ship between autobiography and the novel.

2. Form

Details of the composition of *Les Mots* are both complex and uncertain, and space precludes a full account here.[2] A first draft, of 1953-54, called *Jean sans terre*, was put away until 1961, when Sartre revised it into the text we now have. This draft, written under the influence of Sartre's first spell of fellow-travelling, was evidently much more politically committed; but, since the manuscripts are not available, one can only speculate on what in the final version might belong to this first draft.

At first sight, the obvious way to narrate one's autobiography is the chronological one. Yet on reflexion, this can be seen as simply conventional or even arbitrary. For the *act* of memory, voluntary or involuntary, has nothing to do with chronology; the key factor is affective significance. Again, *pace* certain neo-Freudians, we have no memory of our own birth at all, so to set about in the conventional manner with an account of the circumstances of one's begetting, probably preceded by details of parents and near ancestors, must be somewhat artificial. Such an account cannot depend on genuine memories, only on family tradition in oral or written form. This problem has led critics such as Philippe Lejeune not only to question the whole idea of chronological order in autobiography but to condemn it as a 'solution de facilité' which has run its course and should be superseded.[3]

Yet if the act of memory does not depend on chronology, it is arguable that our interpretation of memories in large part does. The notion of causality is inseparable from that of temporality; and when we try to understand other people's lives, even on the humblest everyday plane, we inevitably put their actions

[2] I have discussed the genesis of *Les Mots* at some length in *15*.

[3] P. Lejeune, 'L'ordre du récit dans *Les Mots* de Sartre', in *5*, pp.197-200. This is probably the most incisive critical study of *Les Mots*.

into some kind of chronological mental order. Otherwise family, social or intellectual background cannot be comprehended. This being so, it seems natural that if we review our own life, we should do so in a similar framework of temporality; and that if we attempt to write about it, we should act in the same way. To say this is not to claim that excellent autobiographies cannot be written except in the chronological mode; clearly they can, and have been. But it is not surprising that most follow the flow of time. Artificial in some ways, granted; but any other narrative method, such as the thematic, may in the end be equally so. The thematic technique, indeed, is usually chronological anyway within the limits of the separate themes introduced. And of course the chronological method does not exclude breaks in sequence such as flashbacks, anticipations, or various kinds of digression. Thus the fact that relatively few autobiographies (or biographies) are narrated in any way but chronologically is not so much evidence of the aesthetic naïvety or timidity of their authors, as of the importance of the temporal in human understanding, and of the overriding need for unity, which is automatically supplied by chronological sequence. On the reader's side, too, the chronological technique will most easily achieve intelligibility and therefore assent.

The form of *Les Mots* is, like most other aspects, both deceptive and ambiguous. The work begins with an expository section dealing with Sartre's family background, his 'prehistory', then the bulk of the text consists of childhood memories overlaid with reflections by the mature adult, with finally another short section in which Sartre discusses his present attitude towards the memories recalled and analysed. Superficially this appears to conform to the chronological, linear approach adopted in the great majority of autobiographies. True, there are no conventional chapters, simply blocks of text, of unequal length, divided by blanks on the printed page. These are gathered into two antithetical 'halves' of the book, entitled respectively 'Lire' (106 pages of text) and 'Ecrire' (96 pages).

The most careful and thoroughgoing analysis of *Les Mots* has been carried out by Lejeune (*5*, p.211), who divides the book not into two but five sections or 'acts':

I.   'Situation et liberté' (pp.11-18)
II. 'Les comédies primaires' (pp.19-72)
III. 'La prise de conscience du vide' (pp.72-95)
IV. 'Les comédies secondaires' (pp.95-175)
V.   'La folie' (pp.175-214)

These are further divided into numerous sub-sections, such as 'prise de conscience de la contingence'. Lejeune's detailed and ingenious analysis is perhaps over-schematic and contrived, but contains a crucial point. This is that despite superficial impressions, the division of the book into the two parts, 'Lire' and 'Ecrire', is not in fact chronological. The events in 'Lire', once the initial expository section is past, can be shown by Sartre's own occasional references to dates or his age to take place between the ages of four and eleven, mostly between six and eleven. Those in 'Ecrire' occur between the ages of seven and eleven, so that this second part of the work overlaps. Writing does not follow reading, but is contemporaneous with it. Lejeune's breakdown of the text underlines this, by making Sartre's own division between 'Lire' and 'Ecrire' fall, not between two of his 'acts', but in the middle of the fourth.

Lejeune thus shows, I think conclusively, that the narrative form of *Les Mots*, superficially chronological, is in reality *thematic* — I prefer this word to the over-used term 'dialectical' — carefully reconstructed by Sartre with hindsight. Looked at another way, in much of the work Sartre is aping chronology as a means of stringing together separate, discontinuous memories. However, this thematic structure is still tied to temporality by the crucial date of 1917, the year of Anne-Marie's remarriage, since all that matters must happen by then. My own conclusion would be that *Les Mots* cannot easily be forced into any formal straitjacket. If it could, much of its richness and density would be lost, since they depend on its inner contradictions, which cannot simply be overcome by 'dialectical' sleight-of-hand. Above all, the last pages are far from a clear and simple 'closed' ending, but are, as we shall see, highly problematical.

The nature of the narrative 'je' is also nowhere near as simple as might at first appear. At one extreme, there is the 'je' of the mature author; at the other, of Poulou at the time of the events narrated. Even this is complex, since there are two 'mature' Sartres involved, and at the Poulou end of the spectrum, not only real memories are involved (or memories of memories), but Sartre's reinterpretation of these, so that the apparent 'je' of Poulou may really be a rhetorical projection of the later Sartre. There is also use of a vague 'on', enabling responsibility to be shifted from Poulou to others unspecified: 'On me montre une jeune géante, on me dit que c'est ma mère' (p.21). In addition, Sartre occasionally jumps from his childhood to intervening points in time, to his years at *Normale* (p.165) or to when he was thirty (p.200). Moreover, though this is true of all auto-biography, the first person narrating events will also have reflected on them, at any time from immediately afterwards to the point of actual composition. This complexity is echoed in the narrative tenses, where the chronological indeterminacy of many events is underlined by use of the imperfect instead of past definite, or where the present and perfect used for musings of the mature Sartre mingle with the same tenses used for past narrative. The result of this slipperiness of the narrative 'je' is inevitably a high degree of confusion between the first person as subject and object, narrator and protagonist, and beneath the apparent chronological narration, onion-skin layers of complexity.

The usual experience of early childhood is that of an eternal present, with extremes of happiness or misery precisely because the child cannot easily see beyond the present, and this is what many autobiographies, motivated by nostalgia, attempt to recapture. However this aspect is largely lacking in *Les Mots*: Poulou is made to be constantly looking foward to the literary career, even posthumous fame, of the adult writer. This perspective is forced on the book by Sartre's method of fitting all the memories he used into a Procrustean pattern. There is indeed no great number of actual memories, although there is no reason to doubt that those related are initially genuine, if subject to inevitable distortion, conscious or unconscious. In fact Sartre did not need to rely on his own recollections alone in composing the book: he was sharing a flat with his mother, conveniently at hand to answer questions. He also had family photographs to help jog his recollections: some of these have been published and were doubtless in his mother's keeping. Letters from the young Poulou, if not examples of his early literary efforts, may too have been available. We should add to these primary sources innumerable echoes, voluntary or otherwise, from Sartre's reading. He was also not above fabrication. It has been pointed out that the dictionary definition of a shark (p.123) is not taken, as Sartre claims, from the *Grand Larousse* of his childhood, but from the *Petit Larousse Illustré* of the 1950s.

However this may be, the way these various sources, narrated with a wealth of rhetorical flourishes, are used, linked, and interpreted, depends entirely on the mature Sartre's aims and preoccupations. Childish they may be in the literal sense, but as encountered by the reader there is nothing naïve about them. What they tell us is what the later Sartre wants us to believe about his childhood, not what it was actually like.

3. Antecedents

Les Mots begins with a deceptively bland sentence: 'En Alsace, aux environs de 1850, un instituteur accablé d'enfants consentit à se faire épicier' (p.11). Here we have what appears to be a factual, historical event, narrated in the *passé simple*. It is of course commonplace in autobiography for the author to provide ancestral background, but matters here are not so simple: right from the start Sartre exploits the conventions of autobiography by both using them and turning them against themselves. The normal tone in narration of background is one of filial piety: Sartre embarks from his first sentence on sustained mockery, undermining all respect for the characters and events presented.

The unexpected phrase, 'accablé d'enfants', creates comic effect, while the casual-sounding expression, 'consentit à se faire épicier' trivializes and ridicules what must have been radical change in a man's existence, indeed one of the most important decisions of his life. The term 'épicier' — whether or not factually true — represents the lucre-grubbing occupation most despised in the nineteenth century by the whole Romantic tradition. Nor is the date fortuitous. As it happens, there is external evidence about what actually occurred. The teacher, Sartre's maternal great-grandfather, in reality lost his post because he refused to swear the oath of loyalty imposed by Napoleon III on all *fonctionnaires*, and had to seek a living in a different field (*25*, p.1066). This change of occupation, far from being somehow contemptible, must have acquired a considerable degree of moral courage.

Seen in this light, Sartre's next sentence takes on a different significance: 'Ce défroqué voulut une compensation: puisqu'il renonçait à former les esprits, un de ses fils formerait les âmes: il y aurait un pasteur dans la famille, ce serait Charles' (p.11). This sentence appears to follow smoothly on the first, but on examination we realize that it does not deal with events, but consists of psychologizing, Sartre guessing, in fact, at motives, using moreover the modern notion of 'compensation'. At the same time he introduces both a key theme and a key motif. The theme is that of *formation*, in its French sense of the moulding of character and values; central to the whole book is the moulding of Sartre's own values by this grandfather. The motif is that of religious vocation: the book is studded with the vocabulary of religion, usually used ironically.

Charles (Karl), the dominant character in the boy's education, is the most memorable character in the book. From the start he is treated satirically: 'Charles se déroba, préféra courir les routes sur la trace d'une écuyère. On retourna son portrait contre le mur et fit défense de prononcer son nom' (p.11). The future pillar of the Third Republic's academic establishment has to have feet of clay, sowing traditional wild oats, pursuing a circus-rider — one stage worse than an actress — and being rejected by his family — 'on' — in an equally stereotyped way. The ironic effect is clear; how much historical truth there is here is more doubtful.

A later sentence gives the clue to Sartre's technique in this opening expository section. We read, of Karl's brother Louis, that 'le père s'empara de ce garçon tranquille et le fit pasteur en un tournemain' (p.11). What we are dealing with is not a factual narrative but a parodic variation of the fairy-tale, with sudden, magical, 'hey presto' developments and reversals, free of the normal constraints of slow-moving time. This is combined with a certain 'throwaway' tone, as when Sartre goes on to dispose of his great-uncle in another single sentence: 'Plus tard Louis poussa l'obéissance jusqu'à engendrer à son tour un pasteur, Albert Schweitzer, dont on sait la carrière' (p.11). So much for the famous missionary: Sartre intends to stand in no-one's shadow, and moves briskly on. The result is a lively narrative, recalling indeed *Candide*, where Voltaire used similar techniques in a purely fictional context; here, as recapitulation of historical fact, the actual lives of human beings, it is pure caricature.

Sartre continues to put his ancestors and relations smartly in their place: he could, after all, say with Vigny: 'Si j'écris leur histoire, ils descendront de moi'. Karl's later adoption of the teaching profession and his marriage to Louise Guillemin are treated in the same vein. The relationship of Sartre's grandparents is indeed antithetical, preparing fundamental ambivalence in his own life: Karl nominally a Protestant, Louise a Catholic become sceptic, Karl German-speaking, Louise French, and her whole attitude to life a negative reflection of her husband's. Sartre pushes this aspect of his grandmother's personality to the point of attributing to her qualities which many have considered typical of himself, 'l'homme du non': 'cynique, enjouée, elle devint la négation pure; d'un haussement de sourcils, d'un imperceptible sourire, elle réduisait en poudre toutes les grandes attitudes' (p.13).

The relationship between the grandparents is presented as another stereotype, the typical present-day view of the archetypal nineteenth-century bourgeois couple, a chauvinist dictatorial husband whose frigid wife was prepared to submit to sex only for purposes of procreation. The upbringing of the resulting children also follows a stereotype. The sons, Sartre's uncles, received an excellent education and adopted professions; Sartre's mother was, however, deprived of any sensible education: 'Anne-Marie, la fille cadette, passa son enfance sur une chaise. On lui apprit à s'ennuyer, à se tenir droite, à coudre. Elle avait des dons: on crut distingué de les laisser en friche; de l'éclat: on prit soin de le lui cacher' (p.15). At least this is how Sartre chooses to present the matter, with the contemptuous 'on' and the usual caricatural foreshortening.

He gives even shorter shrift to his paternal ancestors, in the same mocking parodic style:

> un médecin de campagne épousa la fille d'un riche propriétaire périgourdin et s'installa avec elle dans la triste grand-rue de Thiviers, en face du pharmacien. Au lendemain du mariage, on découvrit que le beau-père n'avait pas le sou. Outré, le docteur Sartre resta quarante ans sans adresser la parole à sa femme; à table, il s'exprimait par signes, elle finit par l'appeler 'mon pensionnaire'. (p.15)

Here of course we have yet another stereotype, the arranged marriage followed by immediate *mésentente* because of trickery over the dowry; with moreover a literary antecedent, the marriage of Charles's parents in the first chapter of *Madame Bovary*. Nor is the allusion to the 'pharmacien' gratuitous: one immediately thinks of Homais. Flaubert was much in Sartre's mind long before *L'Idiot de la famille*. Sartre's father, Jean-Baptiste, is disposed of in equally unceremonious fashion: 'En 1904, à Cherbourg, officier de marine et déjà rongé par les fièvres de Cochinchine, il fit la connaissance d'Anne-Marie Schweitzer, s'empara de cette grande fille délaissée, l'épousa, lui fit un enfant au galop, moi, et tenta de se réfugier dans la mort' (p.16). No conventional display of filial sentiment here. Widowed and without resources, Anne-Marie was forced to return to her family and to play the role of another bourgeois stereotype, the daughter as unpaid housekeeper, back indeed to the status of a minor, at twenty-four.

Thus sketching in all that he wishes the reader to know of his family history, and having by his consistent deployment of mocking irony created the appropriate critical attitude, Sartre makes an immediate transition to his own psychology, admitting that he is ambivalent as to the advantages or disadvantages of the missing father: 'j'ai laissé derrière moi un jeune mort qui n'eut pas le temps d'être mon père et qui pourrait être, aujourd'hui, mon fils. Fut-ce un mal ou un bien? Je ne sais; mais je souscris volontiers au verdict d'un éminent psych-analyste: je n'ai pas de Sur-moi' (p.19). This last remark has become famous, but it need not be taken as gospel. Critics have not been slow to point out that one could scarcely interpret the Freudian notion of the superego, in terms of the compulsion to write, more graphically than by the later Sartre. 'On m'a cousu mes commandements sous la peau: si je reste un jour sans écrire, la cicatrice me brûle (p.139) — a superego in full operation, and an obvious allusion to Kafka's *In the Penal Colony*.

But there is no need to assume the analyst really existed. The introduction of the notion of the superego (one of only three times that Sartre uses actual Freudian concepts in *Les Mots*) may simply be another piece of tongue-in-cheek 'comédie' by Sartre, a rhetorical flourish to serve notice early in his book that he intends to stand no nonsense from *external* psychologizing. If anyone is going to apply Freud to him, he will do it himself. This has naturally not stopped such attempts being made, for example a crude effort by A. James Arnold and Jean-Pierre Piriou to inflict on Sartre a 'Griselda-complex' (2), and more recently a much more sophisticated and seductive study by Josette Pacaly (7).[4]

Sartre moves from consideration of his father to firm judgments on himself: 'Plutôt que le fils d'un mort, on m'a fait entendre que j'étais l'enfant du miracle. De là vient, sans aucun doute, mon incroyable légèreté' (p.20). In this notion we might suspect traces of the common Romantic obsession with circumstances of birth, usually glamorizing the mediocre. This itself is connected with the mythical: in myth, the hero's birth usually falls outside the laws of nature.[5] Later in the book Sartre appears to regret bitterly this same 'légèreté' he is now praising as the basis of his sense of freedom; no matter. What immediately follows is even more dubious: 'Je ne suis pas un chef, ni n'aspire à le devenir. Commander, obéir, c'est tout un' (p.20). How could anyone who for over thirty years by deliberate choice launched into bitter political disputations deny wanting to be a 'chef'? What can this mean except wishing to dominate others, make them subject to one's own will? — unless one assumes that Sartre's compulsive urge, post-1945, towards political commitment was the result of guilt about his apolitical stance pre-war. But then what is guilt but the specific product of the claimed-to-be-missing superego? There is no way out of contradiction here. And a further comment a few pages later is

[4] Freudian enthusiasts can revel in the latter, a perceptive study, where Mme Pacaly gives Sartre the full treatment. She points out that between the first and revised versions of his autobiography, Sartre studied Freud for his ill-fated scenario of the John Huston film (published by Gallimard in 1984). Her conclusion is that about Freud, as so much else, Sartre was typically ambivalent: 'Il n'a pas eu assez de modestie pour se soumettre, dans sa vie, à une méthode élaborée par d'autres, ni assez de force, dans son œuvre, pour ignorer Freud à partir du moment où ce dernier devenait, avec Marx, une des idoles du demi-siècle' (7, p.452).

[5] A comment on Sartre by a friend of Raymond Aron is perhaps apposite: 'pas de père, issu d'une vierge et lui-même Logos'. R. Aron, *Mémoires*, Julliard, 1983, p.36.

little less than breathtaking, if meant seriously: 'pas de Sur-moi, d'accord, mais point d'agressivité non plus' (p.25).

Having dealt summarily with his family and sent psycho-analysis about its business, Sartre has cleared the ground for an equally decisive affirmation about his own nature, and intends to brook no contradiction: 'j'ignorais la violence et la haine [...]. Contre qui, contre quoi me serais-je révolté; jamais le caprice d'un autre ne s'était prétendu ma loi' (p.25). This un-compromising statement is, once more, not easy to reconcile with the general portrait of Karl as domestic dictator. Certainly, until the La Rochelle years, the young Poulou appears not to have rebelled, but if so not because there was no dominant figure in the family against whom revolt was theoretically possible.

Sartre moves on to an obsessive target, the complacent optimism of the Third-Republic bourgeoisie: 'On m'adore, donc je suis adorable. Quoi de plus simple, puisque le monde est bien fait? On me dit que je suis beau et je le crois' (p.26). Now social criticism is one thing, though it is arguable that the pre-1914 *belle epoque* of a France at peace was in some ways more attractive than the régimes which have followed. Linking it to Poulou's own consciousness, via Karl, is another. Surely in the child the feeling of security, of being loved and under the protection of benevolent parental authority, is normally regarded as the desirable ideal, attainable by other social groups than simply a privileged, cosseted minority, while acceptance of this state in the young child will precede any critical rejection of it. What Sartre is in fact doing by this ironical treatment is wishing back his later — much later — political attitudes on to Poulou.

The feeling that all's well in the world is made to inspire in Poulou a conservative sense of the rightness of social divisions: 'tout le monde est bon puisque tout le monde est content. Je tiens la société pour une rigoureuse hiérarchie de mérites et de pouvoirs' (p.30). And in this pyramid, Poulou starts near the top, with a further allusion to *Candide*, as he is shown as admiring 'la chance folle qui m'avait fait naître dans la famille la plus unie, dans le plus beau pays du monde' (pp.31-32). Even the whole notion of Progress is mocked as being no more than a projection of Poulou's self-satisfaction: 'le Progrès, ce long chemin ardu qui mène jusqu'à moi' (p.31). Only Louise is seen as injecting a sceptical note, refusing to be taken in by the boy's play-acting. And the expository section, laying the basis for Poulou's future development through the printed and written word, concludes on this note of complacency about the state of the world, the sense of an eternal present of childhood reflected in the present tense of the narrative.

4. Lire

A key sentence begins the crucial section of *Les Mots* which Lejeune calls the 'comédie littéraire': 'J'ai commencé ma vie comme ja la finirai sans doute: au milieu des livres' (p.37). The tone of mild amusement adopted here was, not the only time in the book, to be turned into one of brutal irony by his own fate: he did indeed finish his life amid books, but for years his blindness had prevented him from reading them.

From birth, Poulou breathed in the atmosphere of authorship, because Karl, having written his own books, was an authenticated 'artisan spécialisé dans la fabrication des objets saints' (p.39). His *Deutsches Lesebuch* produces Poulou's first introduction, in the comic mode, to Marxist economics. Karl's publisher evidently cheated on his royalty statements: 'Je découvris, stupéfait, l'exploitation de l'homme par l'homme' (p.40). Here Sartre's aim is again condemnation of the whole hypocrisy of bourgeois society: 'Sans cette abomination, heureusement circonscrite, le monde eût été bien fait, pourtant: les patrons donnaient selon leurs capacités aux ouvriers selon leurs mérites' (p.40). And the unfortunate Karl is, in a further twist of religious imagery, transformed into Tartuffe: 'ce saint homme'.

This great leap forward into political consciousness is made to precede Poulou's initiation into reading, at a precociously early age. The miraculous broadening of a sensitive child's universe through the printed word is not unique to Sartre, far from it, but, memory assisted by adult imagination, is made to inspire the pattern of his mature thought. Thus his astonishment and delight at discovering that familiar fairy-tales, almost part of the furniture of daily rituals like his bath, could also exist within the covers of a book, and in more noble form, foreshadow the belief in the primacy of words over things. And, by being embodied in print, stories passed from an arbitrary, contingent level to the superior plane of the necessary.

Reading, once he had learned how, was not only the magic key to a superior level of being, but Sartre deliberately makes it responsible for his lack of sensitivity to nature (p.44). In reality we need see here no more than a typical Parisian flat-dweller's childhood, where, holidays apart, the only contacts with 'nature' were chaperoned expeditions to the Luxembourg gardens; the contents of books were naturally more real to Poulou, with their vivid illustrations. Again, this is not an unusual experience among children of a bookish bent, just as is sensitivity to the magic appearance, opacity, and mystery of words not yet understood.

Once more, though, Sartre goes beyond conventional recapturing of childhood experience by linking it to philosophical speculation: to the Platonic Idea, more 'real' than reality; 'au Jardin d'Acclimatation, les singes étaient moins singes, au Jardin du Luxembourg, les hommes étaient moins hommes' (pp.45-46). He continues with an insight into himself which few would deny: 'C'est dans les livres que j'ai rencontré l'univers: assimilé, classé, étiqueté, pensé, redoutable encore; et j'ai confondu le désordre de mes expériences livresques avec le cours hasardeux des événements réels' (p.46).

Where this reader would disagree, however, is in Sartre's next claim, that after three decades he has managed to rid himself of this idealism. He abandoned idealism in aesthetics only to take it up again in politics, in which field his knowledge came yet again not from life but from the printed word. In any case, as usual with Sartre, matters are not quite so simple. In this respect, 'platonicien' he may have been; in others not. The central tenet in his Existentialist philosophy is precisely that existence precedes essence, which may be equated with the Platonic Idea. And existence has to be willed, virtually created *ex nihilo*, without recourse to any pre-existing model.

Karl supplied the key to the arts of music and architecture as well as literature. A crucial passage (pp.52-53) brings together Lamartine, Flaubert and Hugo, in a kind of mystical pantheism, and despite the ironic treatment, this was to be the basis of Sartre's own idealist vocation: faith in Art, specifically

Literature, and one which would outlive his apparent recantation in the closing pages. In an extended metaphor Sartre equates Art, as the summit of human endeavour, with the Schweitzer sixth-floor flat in the Rue Le Goff. This elevated situation takes on symbolical value with, for Sartre, a curiously determinist psychology, since he claims that 'Tout homme a son lieu naturel; ni l'orgueil ni la valeur n'en fixe l'altitude: l'enfance décide' (p.53). So much, again, for Existential choice. Here also, not for the only time, we find an allusion to Camus's *La Chute*, when Sartre goes on to say: 'Longtemps j'étouffai dans les vallées, les plaines m'accablèrent'. Camus devotes a long passage to 'ces points culminants, les seuls où je puisse vivre', including the remark: 'En montagne, je fuyais les vallées encaissées pour les cols et les plateaux'.[6] The demon of parody seems often to have been irresistible; and it is a fair comment that the gratingly ironic posture and tone of the *juge-pénitent* are not altogether unlike those of the narrator of *Les Mots*, who would spend the last years of his life in a tenth-floor tower flat in Montparnasse. Be this as it may, Sartre is explicit in identifying this sense of elevation as the root of his creative dynamic: 'l'Univers s'étageait à mes pieds et toute chose humblement sollicitait un nom, le lui donner c'était à la fois la créer et la prendre. Sans cette illusion capitale, je n'eusse jamais écrit' (pp.53-54). Here we are far from an aesthetic of observation, or even self-expression: literature becomes a form of power-instinct, of domination over the whole world.

Karl's preferred authors were in fact the conventional ones of the earlier nineteenth century, the Romantics; of his contemporaries, only Anatole France and Courteline found favour. Somewhat bitterly, Sartre accuses his grandfather of inflicting on him 'les idées en cours sous Louis-Philippe' (p.56). Since Karl was only three when France's last king was swept away in 1848, this is scarcely fair, but again Karl is turned into a caricature of all Sartre dislikes in the nineteenth century, linking aesthetic values to a general smug, sanctimonious complacency. In reality, as far as teaching was concerned, Karl, far from being some kind of superannuated fuddy-duddy, a dried-up Teutonic

[6] A. Camus, *Théâtre, Récits, Nouvelles*, Gallimard [1974], pp.1487-88.

pedagogue, was a pioneer of new techniques, such as the direct method. Sartre is simply using him as a stalking-horse for an attack on Romantic values, especially the cult of Art as religion-substitute. There is, though, a touch of defensiveness in Sartre's conclusion here: 'Je prenais le départ avec un handicap de quatre-vingts ans' (p.56). Karl, like most of us, could scarcely be expected to have other values than those of his early maturity; and it is difficult to see the young Sartre as anything but a cultural *privilégié*, brought up, like Gide, Proust, or Martin du Gard, on the classics and the books acknowledged as master-pieces at the time. The mechanism of ego-defence is at work once more. The later Sartre — if anything, even more so *after Les Mots* — was still acting out the role of the Artist/Prophet; while much of Existentialism clearly derives from the Romantic belief in intensity of living. Ambivalence yet again: mockery of his Romantic roots cannot free Sartre of them.

The picture of the precocious child manipulated by his grand-father is filled out with another anecdote: Poulou's decision, instigated by Karl, to write to the comic dramatist Courteline. This letter surfaced, not with Sartre's encouragement, in 1950, and deserves quotation in full:

> Cher Monsieur Courteline
>
> Grand-père m'a dit qu'on vous a donné une grande décoration cela me fai bien plaisir quart je rit bien en lisant Théodore et Phanthéon Courcelle qui passe devant chez nous. J'ai aussi esseyé de traduire Théodore avec ma bonne allemande mais ma pauvre nina ne comprnait pas le sence de la plaisentrie.
>
> Votre futur ami (bonne année)
>
> Jean-Paul Sartre 6 ans 1/2[7]

One can sympathize with Sartre's 'agacement' on being con-fronted with this infantile product (of January 1912); he had probably forgotten the whole episode. Courteline, wisely,

[7] Reproduced in ed. M. Contat & M. Rybalka, *Les Ecrits de Sartre*, Gallimard, 1970, p.225.

declined to reply. 'Agacement', indeed, is a key concept in understanding the attitude of this later Sartre to his childhood memories, so alien to the man he wished to have become. Again, a common feeling: how many mature adults can look back on their childhood or adolescence without a single cringe? Neither Sartre's childhood circumstances nor his later attitude to them are unique. After all, the father was missing from countless European homes in 1914-18, and in millions of cases permanently. This apart, Poulou's experience was that of any studious child with few possibilities of entertainment, even of occupation, except a large quantity of books to hand. Whether this is psychologically healthy is a different matter.

At this point Sartre appears to take stock in his narrative, taking up the cardinal question of autobiographical sincerity: specifically, how far what appear to be genuine memories have been overlaid, and in the process distorted, by later reflection.

> Ce que je viens d'écrire est faux. Vrai. Ni vrai ni faux comme tout ce qu'on écrit sur les fous, sur les hommes. J'ai rapporté les faits avec autant d'exactitude que ma mémoire le permettait. Mais jusqu'à quel point croyais-je à mon délire? C'est la question fondamentale et pourtant je n'en décide pas. J'ai vu par la suite qu'on pouvait tout connaître de nos affections hormis leur force, c'est-à-dire leur sincérité. Les actes eux-mêmes ne serviront pas d'étalon à moins qu'on n'ait prouvé qu'ils ne sont pas des gestes, ce qui n'est pas toujours facile. (p.61)

Again the aim is clearly defensive: Sartre anticipates possible critical reactions, admitting awareness of the problem of sincerity, but muddying the issue by refusing to take sides, or rather wanting to have things both ways. At the same time the Existentialist principle enunciated in *Huis clos*, 'Seuls les actes décident de ce qu'on a voulu', is fatally undermined. The question of 'cabotinage' is anyway not only applicable to childhood; human beings imitate and act out roles at all stages of existence, though it is not always clear how far they are conscious of this, and how far such consciousness might modify them. Where Sartre sees Poulou as being in an irredeemably false situation, a child in reality but brought up as an 'adulte en miniature', the experience is not so unusual as he thinks. Practically all children behave in different ways in the presence of adults and among other children. Overprotected and spoiled as he was, Poulou's real problem was not so much his inevitable 'cabotinage' as his deprivation of the peer-group, the world of other children.

Reading itself is assimilated to 'cabotinage'; buried in a volume of Corneille, he was not, as Karl credulously believed, delighting in the alexandrines, but devouring the plot-summaries which conveniently accompanied the plays. To the 'Comédie familiale' Sartre now adds the 'Comédie de la culture', revealing the roots of another fundamental ambivalence. Behind Corneille lay Poulou's *'vraies* lectures', children's illustrated papers and adventure books with his true hero, Pardaillan, bought by Anne-Marie behind Karl's back. These were Poulou's real pleasures, and we catch an authentic note of nostalgia for one of the common joys of childhood, escape into the magic world of Orwell's 'good bad books'. A world moreover in which there are no moral problems, since the villains are all vanquished by the heroes, while violence itself could be rationalized, even idealized, by being, in these heroes with whom Poulou identified, always directed against Evil. Sartre sees in this favourite reading the source of his 'fantasmagorie la plus intime: l'optimisme' (p.66), and ends the section with the admission that he has never lost this taste and would still sooner read a detective novel than Wittgenstein. This is more than an anti-intellectual *boutade*; the later Sartre refused to join in philosophical debate, but simply made affirmations *ex cathedra*. Once again, he seems to be preferring self-accusation here, thus pre-empting external criticism, which might have more bite.

After analysing the joys of reading, Sartre moves, with a jump in real chronology, to his first, failed, attempt at schooling. He was enrolled by Karl in the 'huitième' at the Lycée Montaigne, which would normally be for boys of eight or nine. So far Poulou had received no formal education, not even private tuition. Sartre adopts the comic mode for what must have been a mortifying experience. After his first dictation, strewn with spelling blunders far worse than in the Courteline letter, Karl furiously withdrew him, and Poulou's chance of contact with fellow-children was lost for years. This event, or something like it, evidently occurred, but perhaps the whole episode is coloured by the famous scene in *Vie de Henry Brulard*, where the adolescent Stendhal blotted his copybook by spelling 'cela' as 'cella'. This is not the only scene in *Les Mots* which echoes one from the classical canon of autobiography.

It becomes increasingly obvious that Sartre's main concern is thematic grouping of memories; if their individual sequence happens to be chronological, it is little more than fortuitous. The fundamental experience of 'Lire' turns out to be not so much reading as loneliness, grafted by Sartre on to the meta-physical category of contingency. The world of books, of the imaginary, of fantasy, is what Poulou is thrown back on by inability to escape from solitude.

Sartre moves on from analysis of 'cabotinage' to Poulou's growing realization that the adult Schweitzer world was largely composed of the same thing, and that behind the apparently harmonious bourgeois family lay all sorts of quarrels and disunity. All was in fact not for the best in the best of all possible worlds. Reflecting again on the absent father with a kind of negative nostalgia, Sartre lists the qualities he might have acquired had his father lived:

> Un père m'eût lesté de quelques obstinations durables; faisant de ses humeurs mes principes, de son ignorance mon savoir, de ses rancœurs mon orgueil, de ses manies ma loi, il m'eût habité; ce respectable locataire m'eût donné du respect pour moi-même. Sur le respect j'eusse fondé mon droit de vivre. Mon géniteur eût décidé de mon avenir: polytechnicien de naissance, j'eusse été rassuré pour toujours. (p.76)

This is one of the most ambivalent and paradoxical passages in the entire book. The missing father thus described sounds much less like Sartre's real father than his hated stepfather, Joseph

Mancy, who did indeed take the place of the missing father, but not at all to Sartre's satisfaction. 'Polytechnicien', with 'ingénieur', was for Sartre one of the most opprobrious of terms, here linked with the hardly desirable qualities of 'humeurs', 'ignorance', 'rancœurs' and 'manies', which it is difficult to believe he could genuinely wish on Poulou, simply to remove his sense of alienation. Could he really have wanted a career foisted on him by a domineering father? Even less, the inheritance of wealth: 'M'eût-il laissé du bien, mon enfance eût été changée; je n'écrirais pas puisque je serais un autre' (p.76); again, what happens then to Existentialist liberty? With a peculiar ironic *Schadenfreude* Sartre seems to be coveting the qualities of the bourgeois *salaud* so savagely condemned elsewhere, and the note of yearning is directed precisely at the essence of that *salaud*, his carefree shrugging off of contingency, his belief that, because of his privileges, he is necessary in the world and has a right to exist. The irony is not only internal: it can indeed be argued that Sartre's whole notion of Existentialist liberty depends in large part on his unusually privileged situation.

A tinge of self-pity may perhaps be detected in the anecdote Sartre uses to underline his point: 'Il y a quelques jours, au restaurant, le fils du patron, un petit garçon de sept ans, criait à la caissière: "Quand mon père n'est pas là, c'est moi le Maître". Voilà un homme! A son âge, je n'étais maître de personne et rien ne m'appartenait' (p.76). Some might find this anecdote less admirable than does Sartre, who seems taken in by another obvious form of 'cabotinage': self-assurance is after all a pre-eminently social quality, depending on prior confidence that others will accept one's actions at one's own valuation — the *salaud* again.

*   *   *

The first significant character outside the Schweitzer family is Karl's colleague Simonnot, presented satirically as another exemplar of bourgeois solemnity, as self-satisfied as Karl and equally assured of the necessity of his own existence. Solid even in his absence: at the *fête* of Karl's *Institut des Langues Vivantes*, the missing Simonnot is 'absent en chair et en os', transformed into a metaphysical conceit, pure essence, 'un néant creusé par l'attente universelle' (p.79), superior to his physical form. Here essence primes existence once more: the opposite of Poulou's own feeling of contingency, of being superfluous in a universe not designed specifically for him. The reason for the introduction of Simonnot becomes clear. Pondering on the need for Karl and his ageing academic colleagues to believe in their own necessity, Sartre — approaching their age at the time of writing — sees the reason in their anxiety about mortality, definitive expulsion from this too too solid world. This is at least plausible; and if Sartre is right, he must surely be reading his own anxieties back into his grandfather. So contingency, central in Sartre's philosophy, can be linked to Poulou's anguish at the apprehension of his own mortality — another virtually universal experience among children, and one which many would consider a crucial element in moral education. Thus Sartre's sardonic mockery of the 'vieillards irremplaçables dont la disparition prochaine allait plonger l'Europe dans le deuil et peut-être dans la barbarie' (p.80) takes on a poignant personal air. Religion could perhaps have mitigated Poulou's terror, but although nominally believers, the Schweitzers had, according to Sartre, allowed their religious convictions to become diluted to the point of being no more than hypocritical social convention. Yet again Karl and his family are used as scapegoats, in a scathing attack on the emptiness behind the façade of bourgeois spiritual values. In his derisory dismissal, Sartre forgets Albert Schweitzer; while he is condemning a situation from which he certainly profited — the tolerance, whatever its causes, Karl's Protestant anticlericalism and his wife's scepticism. Would Sartre have preferred them to bring him up in an atmosphere of intolerant bigotry, just so that he would be liberated from metaphysical *Angst*? At any rate, Sartre claims he early broke with religion. Obliged to attend a course of (Catholic) religious instruction, Poulou turned away from piety in pique, after gaining only the silver medal, second prize, in an essay competition. Then, playing with matches, he set alight a rug, and in his guilt felt the eyes of an angry God upon him, for one final time, before his consciousness of divine presence vanished for ever.

This anecdote provides a rare opportunity for an external check on the accuracy of Sartre's memory. In the recently published *Carnets* of 1939-40, never revised by Sartre, we find occasional allusions to incidents used in *Les Mots*. Sartre's reaction in the *Carnets*, despite the inferior (here silver-*paper*) medal, is far from one of disappointment:

> Je suis encore tout pénétré d'admiration et de jouissance quand je pense à cette narration et à cette médaille, mais cela n'a rien de religieux. C'est que ma mère avait copié de sa belle écriture ma composition, et j'imagine que l'impression que j'avais eue en voyant ainsi ma prose transcrite était à peu de chose comparable à l'émerveille-ment que j'ai eu à me voir imprimé pour la première fois.[8]

Different indeed. Again, instead of setting fire to a rug and feeling divine displeasure, in the *Carnets* Poulou puts his match to a lace curtain, and 'ce souvenir est lié au Bon Dieu, je ne sais pourquoi'. It is evident that Sartre has sharpened up his memories to the point of distortion: they now fit into a pattern of which he was certainly not aware in 1939, besides being thoroughly dipped in the pervading irony. The incident, as described in the autobiography, is both more memorable and more definite; yet the very polish of the style, compared with the hesitancy of the *Carnets*, removes it a stage further from a feeling of authenticity, of how things actually happened.

The narrative next assumes an air of pathos, as Sartre moves from the transcendental to the ridiculous. Karl, unbeknown to Anne-Marie, took Poulou, now seven, to have his long wavy hair shorn. Sartre suggests the usual reason for his shoulder-length locks: his mother would have preferred him to be a girl. A photograph of Poulou, as yet unclipped, has been much published, and if Sartre's own description of himself — 'rose et blond, avec des boucles, j'ai la joue ronde et dans le regard, une

[8] *Les Carnets de la drôle de guerre*, Gallimard, 1983, p.93.

déférence affable pour l'ordre établi; la bouche est gonflée par une hypocrite arrogance: je sais ce que je vaux' (pp.26-27) — is slanted to fit his later political stance, there is no denying that Poulou, sailor-suited, appears a smug, horrid, if perfectly ordinary middle-class child. But the effects of the barber's scissors were traumatic, and although Sartre relates the scene in the comic mode, a sense of heartfelt mortification creeps through: 'Mon grand-père semblait lui-même tout interdit; on lui avait confié sa petite merveille, il avait rendu un crapaud' (p.90). The revelation of Poulou's 'laideur' was irredeemable, and after this 'coup de théâtre' even the boy's 'cabotinage' became much more difficult and less successful; his role of 'chérubin défraîchi' was gone for ever. Self-pity now set in with a vengeance, with self-hatred close on its heels. Sartre uses an extended image, taken up several times later in the book, to illustrate Poulou's feeling of contingency: the guilty traveller, with no ticket, questioned by the ticket-collector and attempting, vainly, to justify his presence on the train.

Compensation, or what Sartre calls his spiritual exercises, took the form of daydreams, projecting himself into fantasies as intrepid hero. Typically he turns his mockery on these, not for their puerility, but for their unquestioning acceptance of capitalist ideology: 'Jamais je ne fus plus éloigné de contester l'ordre établi: assuré d'habiter le meilleur des mondes, je me donnai pour office de le purger de ses monstres' (p.98). How the seven-year old Poulou could be expected to be in a position to recognize, let alone challenge, this presumed ideology is unclear; and critics have not been slow to point out that the vision of the knight-errant just as easily fits the later Sartre. The child is father of the man indeed.

Just as 'literature' has been contrasted with what Poulou really wanted to read, adventure comics, the theatre is now compared with another poor man's pleasure, the cinema, then of course still in its pioneering days. Here is another form of 'cabotinage', Sartre posturing as the common man, a rhetorical conceit running through *Les Mots* like a leitmotif. He leads into his evocation of the cinema by an attack on the theatre as another essentially bourgeois institution, symbolizing the tinsel falsity of nineteenth-century society. Typically the passage begins with another concealed literary allusion, to Proust, and the episode of Marcel's first visit to the theatre:

> Les bourgeois du siècle dernier n'ont jamais oublié leur première soirée au théâtre et leurs écrivains se sont chargés d'en rapporter les circonstances. Quand le rideau se leva, les enfants se crurent à la cour. Les ors et les pourpres, les feux, les fards, l'emphase et les artifices mettaient le sacré jusque dans le crime; sur la scène ils virent ressusciter la noblesse qu'avaient assassinée leurs grands-pères. (p.102)

He contrasts the cinema, 'l'art roturier' and its 'inconfort égalitaire', with other, 'higher', art forms, though in fact it is likely that the cinema has played a greater role in 'intellectual' culture in France than in the Anglo-Saxon countries.

The glamour of the cinema can, too, be seen as having a similar attraction as the stage had for the nineteenth-century spectator, if we accept Sartre's claim that the theatre acted as a substitute for extinct glories. He himself admits the cinema's role as a religion-substitute, at the same time as proclaiming it a genuinely popular art-form. This whole section on the silent cinema is a typical example of how Sartre uses memories less for their own sake as nostalgic evocation of a cherished past than as elements in a counter-ideology, his systematic attack on the traditional French bourgeoisie and all its works. *En passant* he also takes a swipe at Gustave Le Bon's popular theory, in *Psychologie des foules*, that all crowds are potentially destructive mobs. To prove his point, he rather oddly reintroduces his dead father as well as Karl, as representatives of the bourgeoisie: 'A feu mon père, à mon grand-père, familiers des deuxièmes balcons, la hiérarchie sociale du théâtre avait donné le goût du cérémonial: quand beaucoup d'hommes sont ensemble, il faut les séparer par des rites ou bien ils se massacrent. Le cinéma prouvait le contraire...' (p.104). No, says Sartre, instead of the destructive potential of crowds, their essence is solidarity, 'adhérence', and in a curious comment, he links this childhood experience of the cinema to a much later episode in his life, his months as prisoner-of-war in 1940-41. What is paradoxical here is that Sartre is directly, and surely consciously, contradicting Roquentin's reaction, in *La Nausée*, to the *autodidacte*'s account of his own feeling of solidarity with his fellow prisoners-of-war in 1914-18, which so infuriates Roquentin that he comes close to making a physical attack on the older man.

The cinema is also used by Sartre as a link between 'Lire' and 'Ecrire'. The content of the films seen by Poulou was much the same world of adventure and heroism as his favourite reading matter, but after watching a film he felt a certain emptiness and desire for violent imitative action on his own part. Jules Verne's Michel Strogoff, for example, was exempt from the torments of contingency and provided a model for an exemplary existence, precisely because he has a 'mandat', a mission. His life is necessary because it is ordered from on high. Poulou, though, could receive no mission from the Czar, and was condemned to an empty repetition of fantasies, thrown back on his own impotence: once again an impostor, 'de trop', 'surnuméraire'.

As a foil to Poulou's fantasies there was the reality principle: other children. It is most significant that Sartre closes 'Lire' with a scene widely praised for its poignancy: Poulou in the Luxembourg gardens, wandering round the various groups of children who were happily playing, living out real, not fantasy, destinies. Each time he approached a group, Poulou was rejected. Searing humiliation is thus the essence of this final scene of the first part of *Les Mots*: Poulou, the 'étranger', excluded, ignored. A somewhat similar scene in *Si le grain ne meurt* shows the young Gide as the victim of other boys' violence; Poulou's experience is if anything even more mortifying, indelibly burnt into his recollections. In the supreme self-confidence of these other children we again see a germ of the bourgeois *salaud*, suffering from no timid doubts about an absolute right to exist.

5. Ecrire

His posture as a hero having disintegrated in the face of reality, Poulou, claims Sartre, now turned in on himself in a further attempt to evade contingency and justify his existence by a self-appointed destiny in literature. Writing, a solitary act in its essence, would enable him to preserve his dreams and at the same time act as compensation for rejection by his peers.

In writing too Poulou was a prodigy, enthusiastically encouraged by Karl, at seven exchanging verse with the old man; imposture again, cries the mature Sartre. There may be a literary allusion in another memory, of Poulou vainly attempting to rewrite La Fontaine's *Fables* in alexandrines: the young Beyle, not yet Stendhal, labouring over alexandrines in a hopeless struggle to write classical tragedy. Prose proved more congenial to both, and Poulou began his literary career by exemplifying what would become one of the cornerstones of Malraux's philosophy of art: that artists do not obtain their inspiration from trying to reproduce reality, but by imitating other artists. Poulou's first attempt was simply a 'plagiat délibéré' of a fantastic story of exotic adventure he had read; such was the power of words that 'tout était forcément vrai puisque je n'inventais rien' (p.121). Here Sartre recalls the paradox of realism: how can the fact that fiction is a product of the imagination, by definition opposed to reality, be reconciled to any notion of aesthetic 'truth'? For Poulou, the words he set down immediately took on 'la densité des choses', so memory, imagination, and truth became fused in his mind, in what he ironically describes as 'écriture automatique', taking a sideswipe at the Surrealists.

Of course, many great writers — Flaubert the first to come to mind — were scribbling away very early in life, if not quite so precociously as Poulou, who thus follows the tradition of the writer whose youthful vocation long precedes having anything worthwhile to write about. He graduated, we are told, from plagiarizing adventure stories to inventing his own, embodying fantasies with himself as hero, facing unheard-of dangers and vanquishing incredible odds. Yet these fantasies brought back a sense of 'angoisse', via the supernatural; Poulou was chilled to the marrow by a fantastic newspaper story, 'Du vent dans les arbres', in which a chestnut-tree mysteriously pushes its branches through the windows of an upstairs sickroom, literally frightening the unfortunate patient to death; there was no rational explanation. The result of this and similar reading was that 'J'eus peur de l'eau, peur des crabes et des arbres' (p.129), a statement pounced on by critics to 'explain' Roquentin's obsession with the chestnut-tree in *La Nausée* or Frantz's hallucination of crabs in *Les Séquestrés d'Altona*. But this type of experience too is not as unusual as Sartre supposes in timorous children who have just learned to read. 'Fairy-stories', such as those so rightly called Grimm, swarming with ogres, wicked fairies, wolves, and such, can be terrifying to the young children for whom they were once thought suitable.

Anne-Marie encouraged Poulou's literary efforts, parading them so that they became another form of 'cabotinage'; Louise, more sceptical, simply commented that at least they kept him quiet. Karl, on the other hand, disapproved of these wild fictions, just as he did of Poulou's comics. Once again he is made a stereotype: the bourgeois horrified at the nightmare vision that his offspring might become that sordid renegade, the dissolute Romantic artist, exemplified by Verlaine, whom Karl had once glimpsed, 'saoul comme un cochon'. This, Sartre says, is why, instead, Karl deliberately tried to divert his ambitions to the academic, with the aim of entering the Ecole Normale Supérieure and acceding via the *agrégation* to the respectability of the secondary teaching profession. But for anyone in Karl's position such hopes for a gifted grandson could only have been standard, and what Karl told Poulou about the danger of a literary career was just Polonius-like good sense: 'Si je voulais garder mon indépendance, il convenait de choisir un second métier. Le professorat laissait des loisirs; les préoccupations des universitaires rejoignent celles des littérateurs: je passerais

constamment d'un sacerdoce à l'autre' (p.133). This was exactly
what Sartre did with his life until his late thirties, and might well
have for even longer, but for the changed circumstances of the
war.

Sartre follows this up with an extended contemptuous flight
of fancy on his likely existence as a solitary provincial *lycée*
professor in Aurillac, whose actual literary career would go no
further than a few futile dilettante endeavours. What Aurillac
had done to deserve such singling out is not clear; it obviously
symbolizes Sartre's own horror of provincial mediocrity and
ennui, much as did the two nearby towns of Ambert and Issoire
in Jules Romains's fantasy, *Les Copains*. Of course it is easy for
Sartre to mock what ought to be a perfectly honourable
pedagogic career, because he himself, Paris-centred like virtually
all French intellectuals, succeeded in avoiding it after a few years
in Le Havre and Laon. Perhaps we may detect not only horror
of the boring trivialities of provincial life, but also uncharitable
feelings, even contempt for those of his fellow-*normaliens*
whose fate it was to pursue such a dull but worthy career. But
after all, for every *normalien* who, like Sartre himself, or a Jules
Romains, or a Pompidou, rose to giddy heights, there are
dozens who live out useful lives, mute and inglorious indeed,
their destiny obscure, in some Ambert or Aurillac, and surely
provincial life is the great gainer.

Sartre's explanation, blaming Karl for his vocation, is
somewhat tortuous, depending at times on direct influence, at
others on Poulou's reaction against such direct influence. Yet
again Sartre is making Poulou out to be much more different
from other intelligent children than he really was. From the
Romantics on, the ideal of the artist's vocation has been conventional in the educated young, however much their bourgeois,
possibly philistine, parents may have dreaded it. Paul Nizan's
background was different from Sartre's in almost every respect;
yet he had the same vocation to write.

With typical ambivalence, Sartre then goes on to contradict
himself anyway, denouncing Poulou's own arrogance — at eight
or ten — for the now detested vocation of writer, in a
memorable outburst of self-disgust as well as hatred for the

milieu he could not escape:

> Et puis le lecteur a compris que je déteste mon enfance et
> tout ce qui en survit: la voix de mon grand-père, cette voix
> enregistrée qui m'éveille en sursaut et me jette à ma table,
> je ne l'écouterais pas si ce n'était la mienne, si je n'avais,
> entre huit et dix ans, repris à mon compte dans
> l'arrogance, le mandat soi-disant impératif que j'avais reçu
> dans l'humilité. (p.140)

It is not easy to understand, rationally, what he wishes the
reader to conclude, especially because, however savage his
attack on the literary vocation, what else could he have wanted?
The obscure career of the dull pedant of Aurillac?   ·

The section which follows (pp.140-75) is considered by
Lejeune the densest of the whole work. It is certainly where
Sartre indulges most intensely in retrospective rationalization;
and in interpreting psychologically Poulou's early attempts at
writing, he largely repeats, in more pithy and striking form, the
analysis of the myth of the bourgeois writer undertaken in
Qu'est-ce que la littérature? (1947). Steeped in irony and parodic
literary allusions, many of these pages are unforgettable.

Sartre interprets Poulou as searching for a necessary *raison
d'être* in life, by identifying the writer as knight-errant, 'je refilai
à l'écrivain les pouvoirs sacrés du héros' (p.142). This quest is
clearly another Romantic notion, and the ideal would be the
writer-hero-martyr: 'mon vrai régiment. Silvio Pellico:
emprisonné à vie. André Chénier: guillotiné. Etienne Dolet:
brûlé vif. Byron: mort pour la Grèce' (p.148). Yet it was not easy
to enlist in this roll of honour: Sartre now attacks the closing
years of the *Belle Epoque* for being unheroic. Even Hugo had
had a tyrant to attack: Napoleon III, and had been persecuted,
as was Zola, another model for the later Sartre. Poulou was thus
a hero without a cause, while Karl is naturally made to shoulder
the responsibility for the next metamorphosis, the artist as
exemplary figure, the lay saint who redeems the rest of humanity
by creating things of beauty. Sartre's present scorn for such
beliefs is unlimited: 'A cause d'elles j'ai tenu longtemps l'œuvre

d'art pour un événement métaphysique dont la naissance intéressait l'univers' (p.151). Thus writing, supremely important, became its own end. So the Romantic sees Art as somehow greater than Life, with the Artist as Demiurge. Or, to use Sartre's own distinction, words implied necessity, while things were merely contingent. Things, in this context, have to include human beings.

Behind this whole development there lies again the Aurillac fantasy, described as the opposite of what was to be Sartre's own Roquentin-like existence in Le Havre. Pursuing a never-to-be-realized bourgeois dream into marriage and material prosperity, Sartre turns it into a savage caricature of Mallarmé, with the Aurillac teacher creating his masterpieces in nightly vigils. From Mallarmé, Sartre's scorn switches back to the Romantics, first Musset, with his belief that Beauty should be created through suffering ('les plus désespérés sont les chants les plus beaux'), then to Vigny's Moïse, the solitary Elect: 'Qu'ai-je donc, Seigneur, pour que vous m'ayez choisi?' (p.157). Sartre provides two different dénouements of the Aurillac fantasy. The first is gloomy, with the unknown author dying, 'sur un lit de fer, haï de tous, désespéré, à l'heure même où la Gloire embouchait sa trompette' (p.159); the second, more optimistic — or less masochistic — for success, fame and the love of women would come to the ageing writer shortly before his death. Sartre now sees a common element in both these fantasized destinies: Art in fact kills Life, 'l'appétit d'écrire enveloppe un refus de vivre' (p.161), and associates this with fear of death.

Writing is thus not only a means of transforming contingency, the intolerable feeling of being 'de trop', into necessity; mortal coils could also be metamorphosed into the eternal, and death itself transcended by posthumous fame. There follows a delightful development of an earlier conceit, the great authors embodied in the actual volumes bearing their name: 'Corneille, c'était un gros rougeaud, rugueux, au dos de cuir, qui sentait la colle' (p.57). Sartre is transmogrified into his complete works, with Assumption into the Heaven of the Bibliothèque Nationale:

aux environs de 1955, une larve éclaterait, vingt-cinq

> papillons in-folio s'en échapperaient, battant de toutes
> leurs pages pour s'aller poser sur un rayon de la
> Bibliothèque nationale. Ces papillons ne seraient autres
> que moi. Moi: vingt-cinq tomes, dix-huit mille pages de
> texte, trois cents gravures dont le portrait de l'auteur.
>   (p.164)

So the vision of survival through Art, Chateaubriand's
Mémoires d'outre-tombe, is both dazzlingly illuminated and
mocked, as is Sartre himself: 'j'ensevelis la mort dans le linceul
de la gloire' (p.164), though pride is not entirely negated by
irony.

Yet a certain sadness pierces through, as Sartre contemplates,
'sans trop de gaîté, la vieillesse qui s'annonce et ma future
décrépitude' (p.165), claiming nevertheless that he is incapable
of visualizing his own death. Meditation on death moves from
the particular to the general, as Sartre considers the lives of great
men. Once across the great divide, they are viewed differently,
and their very death becomes as it were an integral part of their
life, which itself is at the same time transformed from existence
into essence, contingency into necessity: 'Dans les salons
d'Arras, un jeune avocat froid et minaudier porte sa tête sous
son bras parce qu'il est feu Robespierre' (p.169). We learn of
another book which hugely influenced Poulou, entitled
L'Enfance des hommes illustres, and Sartre evokes three
children, Jean-Sébastien [Bach], Jean-Jacques [Rousseau], and
Jean-Baptiste [Poquelin = Molière], while a fourth stands in
their shadow — Jean-Paul [Sartre]! There is a superb arrogance
here, carried off magnificently, but impossible to reconcile with
the rhetoric of the common man.

In the next development, the fundamental ambiguity of
Sartre's entire project is at its most evident. The uneasy and
temporary equilibrium of his vision of himself as great writer
could not last: outside events — the reality principle? — were to
shatter Poulou's personal fantasies. First, the irruption of
history, with the outbreak of war in August 1914. Then, a year
later, the *lycée*, where for the first time he could mix with boys
of his own age. And a third event, undoubtedly the most

important of the three: his mother's remarriage which finally removed him both geographically and psychologically from the Schweitzer milieu.

What we are told of the outbreak of war in 1914 is curiously muted. One might have expected to see — Karl had after all been an exile from his native Alsace for over forty years — a ferment of *revanchard* jingoism. Instead, after a certain initial enthusiasm, we simply see Poulou 'pris en dégoût' because his favourite adventure comics had disappeared from the kiosks, to be replaced by unfamiliar and unwanted war stories in which the individual heroism in which he had earlier exulted was vastly reduced. Dealing with a real war, with its constraints of actual historical fact, and for the first time rereading his 'fantasmes puérils', Poulou was forced to realize that he yet again had become an 'imposteur'. For the duration he gave up writing, but claims that these early war years were the happiest of his childhood. Poulou, now nine, felt at his closest to his mother. One may think this a rosy view inspired by what followed, the real upheaval in Poulou's life. Sartre admits that even while this filial idyll was going on, Poulou had begun to talk to himself: another glimpse of his loneliness, still unable to lead a normal life. Moreover, it was during these years that Anne-Marie, on her side, made the momentous decision to remarry, hardly a sign she was totally satisfied with the status quo.

In any case this intimacy could not last; in October 1915, Poulou, now ten, was finally forced out into the real world, the junior section of the Lycée Henri IV. 'Enfin j'avais des camarades!' (p.186). Not surprisingly, much of the narrative here, describing schooldays and classmates, rejoins conventional autobiographical accounts. And with this joyful human contact with his peers, the sensation of contingency evaporated. That writing 'novels' itself had stopped, confirms the idea that it was largely a form of compensation for the cloistered life forced on Poulou hitherto. Yet Poulou's psychological problems were not permanently solved, claims Sartre in an unexplained jump in the argument. Again using the unnamed analyst friend as a device to permit self-diagnosis, he maintains that far from being cured of the infection of contingency and of the fantasy of conjuring it through writing, he had merely internalized it.

There follows a full-scale assault on the very notion of optimism. First in Poulou himself, in his absolute conviction that he was destined to literary *gloire*: 'mes infortunes ne seraient jamais que des épreuves, que des moyens de faire un livre' (p.196), a curious echo of Mallarmé's 'tout, au monde, existe pour aboutir à un livre'; and one need not stress the religious overtones in this aesthetic version of predestination. The attack on Poulou's belief in his own star as embryo Illustrious Author is then broadened to yet another general onslaught on the facile optimism of the Third Republic, its belief in gradual improvement in general prosperity through education and hard work. Sartre's irony is all the more bitter for being displaced from its primary source, his own optimism of the 1930s, the blind conviction that, come what might in the political arena, he could carry on with his literary career and private life without interruption.

*   *   *

The impression left by the last thirty pages of the book is one of speeding-up of the narrative tempo, a certain breathlessness and confusion very different from the assured tone of the earlier sections. It is not so much a matter of maintaining the reader's interest as the narrative rushes towards its climax, as of controlled irony giving way to self-contradiction in a welter of disjointed affirmations. By the end Sartre indeed appears prepared to say virtually anything if he can express it in a striking formula, unworried about its compatibility with either his own life or what he has earlier written in the same book. Thus, 'J'ai toujours mieux aimé m'accuser que l'univers', he maintains (p.197), a breathtaking claim when one considers that throughout he has been holding others, notably Karl, responsible for his entire vocation, and that most of his later life consisted of a long series of 'J'accuse!'.

At this point evocation of memories ends, and it is left to Sartre to develop his peroration. This he opens by defining Poulou in strictly deterministic terms, very far once more from any notion of Existential choice. The idea of culture, he repeats, is no more than a debased substitute for transcendental religious belief, while *gloire* itself is seen as an equally debased substitute for salvation, posthumous literary fame replacing the lost dream of personal immortality. As a result, Sartre now claims to see his literary ambitions as a vast delusion. But the transcendental remained in the internalized urge to write.

Here Sartre goes on to describe his pride in *La Nausée*, justified pride, indeed, but not exempt from vanity:

> Je réussis à trente ans ce beau coup: d'écrire dans *La Nausée* — bien sincèrement, on peut me croire — l'existence injustifiée, saumâtre de mes congénères et mettre la mienne hors de cause. *J'étais* Roquentin, je montrais en lui, sans complaisance, la trame de ma vie; en même temps j'étais *moi*, l'élu, annaliste des enfers...
>
> (p.211)

'Madame Bovary, c'est moi.' Here we may pause. *La Nausée* was an unqualified success, and perhaps as long as success lasted Sartre indeed felt saved. But by the 1950s, although he was by now famous, nevertheless the major fictional project of his life, *Les Chemins de la liberté*, unfinished — unfinishable? — had been much less warmly received, and the subjective conviction of salvation may have turned to ashes in his mouth. Not only that, but in *La Nausée* Sartre was at his furthest from what he claims he has now become; the whole thesis of *Les Mots* implies forcing human life into an *ex post facto* pattern of the kind Roquentin comes to scorn, abandoning his biography of Rollebon and denying validity to the notions of adventure and privileged moments. Ambivalence through and through.

It is at this point that Sartre introduces the most problematic feature of the whole book, the famous 'adieu à la littérature'. In this, denouncing his whole literary vocation, he denies any value to art:

> depuis à peu près dix ans je suis un homme qui s'éveille, guéri d'une longue, amère et douce folie et qui n'en revient

pas et qui ne peut se rappeler sans rire ses anciens errements et qui ne sait plus que faire de sa vie. [...] Longtemps j'ai pris ma plume pour une épée: à présent je connais notre impuissance. [...] La culture ne sauve rien ni personne, elle ne justifie pas. (p.212)

These well-known lines raise many questions. Their most curious feature is in fact a resemblance to a similar renunciation and denunciation of literature at the end of a work by Jean Guéhenno, *Journal d'un homme de 40 ans* (1934). This, another autobiography, by a poor boy who had hoisted himself up to the Ecole Normale Supérieure more or less by his own bootstraps, ends with a remarkably similar passage:

J'ai trop rêvé. [...] Les livres m'ont un temps tourné la tête. J'espère maintenant être tout à fait désenivré. Je sais que la dignité ne s'apprend pas dans les livres. Innombrables sont les hommes cultivés et pourtant indignes. La culture, dès qu'elle est sentie comme un privilège ou un intérêt, avilit aussi bien que la possession de titres de rente.[9]

This cannot be a coincidence. Guéhenno, one of the most prominent left-wing French writers of the 1930s, was very much in Sartre's mind during that period. At the time he appeared a considerable literary figure (less so in retrospect) and, as a fellow-*normalien* as well, was a natural target for Sartre's envy. He is indeed even attacked by name in *La Nausée*, while his frail physique and humanitarian socialism are awarded to the *autodidacte* and cruelly satirized.

In view of this, we need no longer wonder why Sartre did not indeed abandon literature after 1964, or make any significant change in his way of life. It is clear that the 'adieu' is above all another, breathtaking, example of parody, a rhetorical, purely literary device to provide a neat closure to the book, one which precisely because of its parodic, therefore ironic, overtones cannot be charged with insincerity. It is also further proof, if

[9] J. Guéhenno, *Journal d'un homme de 40 ans*, Grasset, 1934, p.254.

this is needed, that Sartre in the 1960s was still living in a world
not of real life, but of books, of words, including other people's
words, and the 'adieu' just another deployment of words, of
rhetoric, of a deliberately 'literary' technique.

By the use of the 'adieu' Sartre also manages to give a new
twist to autobiographical convention. Usually, autobiographies,
written in the later part of the writer's life, are essentially
backward-looking, as the writer considers the events of his past
in a tone normally reflective and passive. The conventional
authorial stance at the end of an autobiography is that of the
wisdom and serenity of maturity, if not of old age. Of course it
is easy to argue that maturity ensures neither wisdom nor
serenity, even that the mere passing of years does not necessarily
imply maturity. So to this extent this convention may itself be
highly artificial. But the dénouement it provides is one of
peaceful resolution and finality, and the reader can assume that
nothing else of sovereign importance to the author — death
apart — is likely to happen. Sartre's position is different. The
'adieu' allows him to give the impression that he is not now
looking backwards, but is firmly turned towards the future,
active, forward-looking and progressive — even at the cost of
having to admit that he has been entirely wrong about the
central preoccupations of his life until then. This aspect of the
'adieu' invites a comparison with other works, *La Nausée*,
L'Enfance d'un chef, or the final Mathieu section of *La Mort
dans l'âme*, where an individual also investigates his past only to
have a sudden intuitive conversion to completely new behaviour.
This we may see as less a manifestation of Existential choice
than an attempt to rationalize a fundamental instability,
irrationality, in Sartre's own personality.

So despite its self-assurance the famous renunciation of
literature turns out to be a 'faux dénouement', a gesture to give
focus to Sartre's account of his childhood, but as shot through
with ambivalence as anything else in *Les Mots*. The text itself is
moreover typically ambiguous. Despite the firm tone of the
extracts quoted above (p.212), intervening remarks are much
more equivocal: 'J'ai désinvesti mais je n'ai pas défroqué: j'écris
toujours. Que faire d'autre? [...] je fais, je ferai des livres; il en

faut; cela sert tout de même. [...] mon imposture, c'est aussi mon caractère: on se défait d'une névrose, on ne se guérit pas de soi' (pp.212-13), which brings us back to the vision of Sartre slogging away for another decade at the unfinished Flaubert. Now this blurred effect may be partly due to the book's being substantially rewritten, but blurred it is; and the implied appeal to political involvement is equally questionable.

There are other difficulties. Sartre explains his earlier life away as a 'névrose', but does not wish to deny value to the product of that 'névrose', *La Nausée*, which means he is trying to have his cake and eat it. Yet he admits that the mirage of political action — which in his case, in the late 1940s *preceded* even the first draft of *Les Mots* — may itself be another form of 'névrose'. Politics, into which he launched himself with all the intolerance of the convert, would be no better substitute for transcendental religious belief than literature as a defence against mortality. Moreover, Sartre's apparent importance in the political field always depended on his earlier purely literary reputation. (If the names of Chateaubriand and Hugo have gone down to posterity, it is not by virtue of their political careers.) And all the evidence is, from *La Nausée* and *Le Mur* as well as his later career, that what he internalized into writing was not only his 'folie', his 'névrose', but a prodigious aggressivity, the conviction of being always and absolutely in the right. Here we see writing itself as an ego defence-mechanism; self-criticism in *Les Mots* is inspired less by an idea of regret or remorse than by the desire to maintain the ego intact. Thus the very fact of Sartre writing about his 'névrose' may be seen as another symptom of it, and his trenchant affirmations, far from cutting short psychological speculation, merely feed its fires.

The meaning of the last paragraph of *Les Mots* has also puzzled critics. Certainly, in a book so tightly written, with so sustained a rhetoric, we have to assume that Sartre attached considerable importance to the *envoi*, which will be truly a valediction, in no way throwaway. Above all Sartre is concerned with projecting the image of himself as Everyman:

Ce que j'aime en ma folie, c'est qu'elle m'a protégé, du

premier jour, contre les séductions de 'l'élite': jamais je ne
me suis cru l'heureux propriétaire d'un 'talent': ma seule
affaire était de me sauver — rien dans les mains, rien dans
les poches — par le travail et la foi. Du coup ma pure
option ne m'élevait au-dessus de personne: sans
équipement, sans outillage je me suis mis tout entier à
l'œuvre pour me sauver tout entier. Si je range l'impossible
Salut au magasin des accessoires, que reste-t-il? Tout un
homme, fait de tous les hommes et qui les vaut tous et que
vaut n'importe qui. (pp.213-14)

Could Sartre really believe this himself for one minute? From his
own account, the notions of 'élite' and 'talent' were inescapable
elements of his childhood; far from being 'sans équipement,
sans outillage', he was intellectually privileged by his family
background (whatever its psychological drawbacks) and his
education, to an extraordinary degree. And Sartre as the
ordinary man runs counter to almost every notion we have of
him, whether from his own other writings or the observations of
others.

False modesty or not, Everyman is clearly the ultimate image
Sartre wishes his reader to have, and so it remains as the final
example of the ambivalence of the whole work. He may have
wished to exorcize the spectre of *orgueil*; but it is also an allusion
to La Bruyère's (equally disingenuous) 'je suis peuple'. Sartre
thus ends his book with a series of rhetorical flourishes in which
aesthetic intention overrides any commitment to authenticity.
First the 'Adieu to Literature' which is neither original nor
genuine; now the attempt by the 'hypocrite auteur' to claim
identification with the reader, 'mon semblable, — mon frère'.

Another problem here is that Sartre constantly assumes
Poulou was a special case, that his experiences were radically
different from those of the ordinary (dare one say 'normal'?)
child. This may be a facet of Sartre's fundamental narcissism
but even where Poulou's childhood could be reconciled with the
rhetoric of Everyman, it is erected into something *falsely*
unique. We have seen that some of these experiences must be
common to all children, or if not universal, far from rare. Their

description is possibly all the more convincing because readers can and do identify with them, no doubt part of the popular appeal of the book.

What is certain is that, if Sartre were really just anybody, the whole point of his autobiography would evaporate: Poulou's childhood and vocation make sense only in the context of his exceptional destiny, Sartre's fame as a writer. Hence the constant allusions to the childhood of great artists, while the recurrent Aurillac fantasy of dreaded mediocrity, conjured up with such studied contempt, takes on full meaning only in contrast to Parisian literary renown. Sartre is thus more dependent than most autobiographers on his own celebrity. The constant comparisons with the great, not only artists but generals — 'Napoléon, Thémistocle, Philippe Auguste, Jean-Paul Sartre' (p.174) — are made less strident by their irony, but are too insistent to be passed over as entirely tongue-in-cheek. Sartre's implicit *orgueil* is truly monstrous.

6. Motifs

The most vigorously portrayed character in the work is clearly Karl Schweitzer, elevated into a masterly satirical figure. Such is the power of first-person narrative to compel assent that critics have taken the portrait as absolutely authentic. Yet it would be wrong to accept the depiction of Karl here as what Professor Schweitzer was really like, or even what Sartre thought he was really like. The unremitting hostility shown towards him seems like a 'règlement de comptes', and no doubt Sartre felt some genuine resentment. But there are signs that this antagonism was largely retrospective. Sartre wrote respectful letters to Karl until well into his twenties, besides nominating him, not his mother or stepfather, as next-of-kin in his *livret militaire*. We may suspect that the Karl of *Les Mots* attracts in large part hostile feelings displaced from their original target, the detested stepfather. The happiest years of Sartre's childhood were, after all, spent as a 'petit prince' in the Schweitzer household, whatever he may write about it here.

At the same time Sartre skates over aspects of Karl's personality of which he was perfectly aware. Throughout Poulou's childhood years, Karl was having affairs with female students, past and present. This is indeed hinted at in the text, but at something of a tangent. This extra-mural sexual activity must have been one of Karl's major preoccupations, since, incredibly, it was to continue until he reached a state of complete senility at ninety. One can only speculate as to why Sartre should have largely omitted this aspect, on the surface good ammunition for his sustained attack; perhaps he felt it would damage the precise vision he wished to project. It certainly adds a new perspective to the coolness between Louise and her husband, and explains her attitude of disabused scepticism. It also leads to another consideration. Karl, living at Meudon, then in Rue Le Goff, was out at work all day, and thus could scarcely have been at all times the pervasive domineering presence we assume from the book. The influence of Anne-Marie, if not Louise, must have been correspondingly greater. There are other signs that the Karl of *Les Mots* is to a large extent a product of Sartre's creative imagination. There are a number of references to his great age and to his obsession with approaching death. Now this may well have been the case, although the boy Poulou could scarcely know. In the Poulou years Karl was still in his sixties, and obviously very active.

Professor Schweitzer is firmly anchored in the nineteenth century by being bestowed physical characteristics of Victor Hugo in old age. Photographs do show a certain resemblance, but no more than to any other bearded patriarchal figure. But this is less important than the values and attitudes he is made to personify, above all his 'cabotinage' which puts into relief Poulou's own. Karl is thus made into a kind of French Victorian paterfamilias, oozing complacency and moral blindness, a monster of hypocrisy. An exemplary figure of how not to live, of 'mauvaise foi' under full sail, he acts as a target for Sartre's self-hatred and condemnation of his entire childhood, and the aesthetic attitudes it engendered.

Now this aspect of Karl will be far from unfamiliar to English readers, to whom such broadside attacks on hypocrisy are common, as in *The Way of All Flesh* or *Eminent Victorians*. In the end, what we have in Karl Schweitzer is a deliberately constructed literary character, a burlesque caricature, a super-Homais figure designed to act as a focus for the preoccupations and grievances of the mature Sartre. The Homais comparison is not gratuitous. In creating Homais, Flaubert gathered together various strands of his dislike and contempt for the provincial *petite bourgeoisie*, and Sartre could follow the example. As such, Karl belongs to fiction, a splendid creation with a life of his own which almost transcends the covers of the book. He also fulfils an important functional role in the narrative, as the authoritative older figure who holds the story together, since Poulou is inevitably in his shadow throughout. This points to another, aesthetic, reason why the autobiography should end where it does: for it to continue after Poulou and his mother had left the Schweitzer household could only have been an anti-climax in the absence of the dominant character.

Unity is usually not in fact a major preoccupation of the autobiographer, since, whether or not a chronological technique is adopted, the narrative will necessarily be unified by its primary subject, the life and personality of the author. In *Les Mots*, however, the thematic development of 'Ecrire/Lire', ending with the 'adieu', provides a keen sense of pattern and unity, indeed lending the picture of Poulou's life an aura of compelling necessity on first reading, while the work's tight-knit texture has received general admiration.

Sartre's other principal means of binding the narrative together is the systematic use of criss-crossing motifs. Most pervasive is the religious imagery, from the description of the primary ancestor, the great-grandfather, as 'Ce défroqué' in the second sentence of the first page, to the allusion to 'impossible Salut' in the penultimate sentence of the last.

Scarcely a page is not impregnated with such vocabulary, which goes far beyond being simply a literary conceit. Indeed, this imagery can be accused of disintegrating under its own weight, since Sartre has to be in turns disciple, priest, crusader, martyr, and saviour. It both exemplifies and symbolizes the major theme of the book, his long-standing belief in and ultimate rejection of Art as religion-substitute. It is this which gives the work its underlying seriousness, since if Art acts primarily as a psychological defence against mortality, *Les Mots* — the very title may be equated with 'Le Verbe' and thus given fundamental biblical connotations — can be seen as in large part a meditation upon death. A comment from 1960 is apposite: 'je l'ai choisi [ce métier] contre la mort et parce que je n'avais pas la foi'.[10] In this perspective, other remarks fall into place, such as the Pascalian *frisson*: 'aujourd'hui encore, désenchanté, je ne peux penser sans crainte au refroidissement du soleil' (p.209). This not uncommon sentiment can obviously be linked to Poulou's feeling of intolerable metaphysical solitude in a world bereft of God.

Transcendental belief in Art places Sartre squarely in the

[10] *Situations*, IX, Gallimard, 1972, p.32.

Romantic tradition which inspired the aesthetic of many of the greatest French writers: Flaubert and Mallarmé, then Proust, Martin du Gard, and Malraux in our own century. However, Sartre attempts to place himself above such names, by claiming to renounce literature and thus prove greater lucidity. Of course Art can never in truth replace religion, as Mallarmé, whose entire creative endeavour has to be seen in this light, wryly commented: 'Mais ratés, nous le sommes tous! Que pouvons-nous être d'autre, puisque nous mesurons notre fini à un infini?'.

The next most important motif is that of 'comédie', a term used interchangeably by Sartre with that of 'cabotinage', though the latter term has more pejorative overtones, and indeed 'singerie' is at times substituted. 'Cabotinage' has no single equivalent in English, containing as it does components both of vanity and mediocrity, though 'play-acting' is perhaps adequate when applied to a child. For Sartre, in 'comédie' as in 'cabotinage' there is an element of falsity, reprehensibility — the roots of *mauvaise foi*? We should not forget Daniel's outburst in *L'Age de raison*, at a moment of extreme self-disgust: 'Salaud! lâche et comédien: salaud!'.[11] (Malraux uses the same concept, in a somewhat different way: 'l'arme la plus efficace d'un homme, c'est d'avoir réduit au minimum sa part de comédie', we read in *Les Noyers de l'Altenburg*.)[12]

'Cabotinage' in Poulou is treated without indulgence, but for children, especially lonely children, to take refuge in play-acting is a banality, including all forms of day-dreaming, so Poulou's construction of a heroic world round his fantasies is in no way very unnatural. The apparent narrator of any autobiography is of course always a *persona* or comic mask, keeping the reader at arm's length. Thus Sartre, as we have noted, indulges in rhetorical pirouettes of make-believe, such as when, still in his fifties, he alludes to 'le vieillissement qui me délabre' (p.203), or in the vision of himself, totally blind, painfully scrawling his final work. That here is an element of conjuring away fate does

[11] *Œuvres romanesques*, Gallimard, 1981, p.695.

[12] A. Malraux, *Les Noyers de l'Altenburg*, Gallimard, 1948, pp.49-50.

not alter the presence of 'cabotinage', attitudinizing, in such fantasies; nor does the cruel irony that, far from being conjured away, physiological disaster was to be Sartre's destiny. The term of 'comédie', posturing, has to be applied to much of Sartre's later public life, or to his stance as Everyman, and what indeed are Sartre's favourite techniques of parody and pastiche but forms of 'singerie'?

Other motifs are centred on Karl, notably the attack on 'Belle Epoque' optimism, locking him in the best of all possible worlds as the archetypal representative of the Third Republic, each damning the other beyond redemption. The recurrent vision of the train-traveller without a ticket, on the other hand, is focused on Sartre himself, closely connected with the notion of metaphysical contingency. It recalls too the necessity but impossibility of the 'mandat' — vocation raised to the level of divinely appointed 'mission' —, admittedly Kafkaesque in inspiration, and indeed itself possesses some of the qualities of a Kafka parable. Above all, on its last appearance it prepares the climax of the narrative immediately after the narrator's awakening from his thirty years of 'folie' (p.212).

Other images are perhaps little more than imaginative developments, exuberant flights of fancy, even whimsy, such as the Jules Verne-like vision of Sartre as balloonist and deep-sea diver (p.54), especially apt as it links him with the adventure stories at the basis of many of Poulou's fantasies. Even this may of course lend itself — be intended to lend itself? — to psychological speculation, like others such as the repeated images of mirrors — reflecting Sartre's narcissism? —, or of ingestion/digestion/excretion. The more important motifs, though, constantly pointing to underlying significance behind the surface of events, implicitly control and order the narrative, imposing on it the systematic, complex network of corrosive irony.

7. Style

The question of style is obviously paramount in *Les Mots*. Sartre outlined his aims in 1971: 'Le sens du style dans *Les Mots*, c'est que le livre est un adieu à la littérature: un objet qui se conteste soi-même doit être écrit le mieux possible.'[13] Since the notion of the 'adieu' is itself highly contestable, it is not surprising that the whole issue is one of considerable ambivalence. 'Je me disais parfois que je serais sauvé de l'oubli par mon "style"', comments Sartre (p.137), only to deny it two pages later. Jacques Lecarme has commented that two contrasting styles rub shoulders in *Les Mots*, 'un langage noble, cérémonieux, lettré, qui correspond à la religion mais aussi aux mythologies et à la tradition littéraire', and 'un langage dru, plébéien' (*25*, p.1057). We know from Simone de Beauvoir that Sartre used a deliberately formal, 'classical' style, inspired by Gide, Valéry, and Alain, until liberated while rewriting *La Nausée* by reading Céline. Both styles, one should note, are derivative. Thus in *La Nausée* and *Les Chemins de la liberté*, the distinguishing mark of style is negative; it is rather an 'anti-style', composed of hostility to the conventionally beautiful, deliberate lingering over the sordid, shot through with parodic elements and therefore irony.

By the time of *Les Mots*, the irony and parody have come to the fore, with the sordid largely suppressed. The formal style has returned, but is now highly self-conscious, solemnity as a target for irony, with occasional popular language in deliberate contrast. This we may link to the rhetoric of the 'common man', as if popular language, 'plain-speaking', is somehow more 'truthful' than mandarin style. In practice both are in their way artificial, while desire to shock, 'épater le bourgeois', has a long history, not always admirable. Quite rightly Sartre uses vulgarity

[13] *Situations*, X, Gallimard, 1976, p.94.

only sparingly, so as not to spoil its effect, which is usually to puncture pretensions: 'Et puis mon grand-père se plaît à emmerder ses fils' (p.28); 'La petite fille s'en foutait: c'était un ange' (p.120).

A common technique is the use of familiar expressions in an unfamiliar context, and many of the best comic effects are drawn from incongruous juxtaposition: 'Un soir, [Karl] annonça qu'il voulait me parler d'homme à homme, les femmes se retirèrent, il me prit sur ses genoux et m'entretint gravement' (p.133); 'J'avais deux raisons de respecter mon instituteur: il me voulait du bien, il avait l'haleine forte' (p.69). The result is usually satirical, belittling: Sartre's father, 'un mari qui n'avait pas fait d'usage' (p.17); 'en filant à l'anglaise, Jean-Baptiste m'avait refusé le plaisir de faire sa connaissance' (p.19). Sometimes, even, incongruity is pushed a little far, as when Sartre compares his inner compulsion to write with 'ces crabes préhistoriques et solennels que la mer porte sur les plages de Long Island' (p.139), an image deriving from his 1945 American trip but not one which would convey much to the average French reader. Again, desire to shock may be taken to the limits of good taste: 'j'étais une femme froide dont les convulsions sollicitent puis tentent de remplacer l'orgasme' (pp.174-75).

Les Mots comes to a close well before the onset of puberty, so that the question of adolescent sexuality scarcely arises. Poulou is deemed completely innocent, or ignorant, in sexual matters, which Freudians might see as disingenuous suppression of essential facts. There are however a number of allusions to sexuality itself. Some are evidently stylistic, part of the intent to shock. Procreation however attracts curious treatment. First, Karl and Louise: 'Il lui fit quatre enfants par surprise' (p.14); then grandfather Sartre, his wife both unspoken to and unnamed: 'Il partageait son lit, pourtant, et, de temps à autre, sans un mot, l'engrossait' (p.15). Sartre's own parents' sexual relationship comes in for equally short shrift. One does not need to be a Freudian to see in such language a possible reflection of Sartre's own distaste for the idea of procreation; but at the same time it satirizes supposed bourgeois sexual repression and hypocrisy, consciously and deliberately, which is not too easy to reconcile with the idea of its being *un*conscious revelation of Sartre's own neurotic traits.

The general briskness of narrative has obvious consequences. Above all, it largely avoids the pitfall of sentimentality, since practically all experiences described are simultaneously undermined by irony, leaving little place for nostalgia, one of the most common weaknesses in run-of-the-mill autobiographies. Yet, as we have seen, there are exceptions, as in the evocation of Poulou's semi-illicit visits to the cinema with Anne-Marie. Less desirable sentiment also emerges, in the negative form of pathos, self-pity, in the traumatic scene where the boy is rejected by the other children in the Luxembourg gardens.

At other times one may feel that Sartre's very ability to make memorable remarks and coin laconic epigrams leads him into doubtful claims. In such neat formulations, the attraction of the lapidary form may explain their presence, not their truth or falsity. Thus, 'L'enfance bourgeoise vit dans l'éternité de l'instant', he comments (p.80); but this is surely true of all, not just bourgeois, children. It is equally difficult to accept Sartre's corollary, 'c'est-à-dire dans l'inaction'; inaction, the passive state of Gidean *disponibilité*, seems more a product of adult *ennui*.

It is perhaps better to speak, not of two, but of a whole range of styles, of levels of meaning. What this means in practice is that Sartre should always be at least one step ahead of even the most perspicacious reader. No innocuous-looking phrase can be taken purely at face value: it may be a parodic literary allusion, an echo or anticipation of other remarks in this book, or contain a double, even treble, meaning. Thus relatively few descriptive traits are present, and when brief physical notations are included, they may well have been selected not because they stuck in Sartre's memory but for ironical effect. The narrative mode, elliptical and allusive, belongs primarily to the fable, not to realism. As Geneviève Idt, one of the sharpest commentators of this aspect of Sartre, has remarked, it is as if 'tout dans ce livre était entre guillemets' (*20*, p.77). The ideal would perhaps be for every statement in the book to contain at another level its own negative. Certainly each sentence, each paragraph attains its full significance only when taken in conjunction with other sentences and paragraphs in the book, and also in the light of the whole tradition of European literature. In this respect the work is supremely ambitious, and written with consummate self-assurance when we consider that its overt message is, para-doxically, that its author was not only wrong but wasted his time for three decades, half a lifetime, on — literature.

Thus the whole work is intended to be a tightly interlocking artefact of extreme density, a kind of watertight masterpiece, or, to change the metaphor, like a sparkling cut diamond, virtually invulnerable to abrasion, or criticism, from outside because it is harder itself. To use Sartre's own term, 'totalizing'. Under the microscope of detailed textual examination it proves to be con-structed of systematic irony and ambiguity. At this level, *Les Mots* is in fact an ideal model for a type of criticism which has recently become fashionable: 'deconstruction'. It is a work which takes its own assumptions and affirmations to pieces at the same time as it makes them. It is arguable, of course, that in the end a work which does this is not so much self-deconstructing as self-destructing; and, against deconstruction as a general critical principle, that if all literary works challenged themselves in this way, they would all be structurally similar, whereas *Les Mots* is obviously *sui generis*, a monumental *tour de force* of irony. It also is clearly not 'about' language itself, but has a subject securely anchored in Sartre's narcissism.

The effect is, nevertheless, that the attentive reader cannot sit quietly, but is at once provoked and fascinated, constantly alert for allusions and double meanings, or, to use another recently-coined term, the 'sous-texte', which means much the same as the traditional English expression 'reading between the lines'. Here we come back to the notion of irony and ambiguity as self-defence.

It would be tedious to attempt to list, even count, all the literary and cultural allusions, overt and covert, in *Les Mots*, and one could have little confidence that the list was remotely complete. What is certain is that few books of this length could rival it in this respect. Many of these references are explicit and clear, such as an epigraph from Chateaubriand: 'Je sais fort bien que je ne suis qu'une machine à faire des livres' (p.140). The book is studded with such direct allusions, or only nominally concealed, not only to artists, but to the great names of history generally. Alongside runs another series of names, the representatives of the 'low', popular tradition presented as being Poulou's true preference: Pardaillan, the Man in the Iron Mask, the androgynous Chevalier d'Eon, the heroes of Jules Verne. All these names are obviously still alive in the mature Sartre's mind — evidence of the survival of childish hero-worship in adult ambitions?

On a second level there are the hidden or semi-hidden allusions, accessible only to an élite of sophisticated readers: a mandarin technique which belies the notion of the Sartrean narrator as the ordinary man. Thus we read: 'un enfant gâté n'est pas triste; il s'ennuie comme un roi. Comme un chien' (p.81). An innocent-looking series of phrases, though the last two reflections seem unlikely to have been Poulou's own. Behind them, though, 's'ennuyer comme un roi', is an allusion to a famous passage on 'divertissement' in Pascal's *Pensées*. 'Comme un chien' is evidently another example of the self-disparaging motif of Poulou as 'caniche'. But 'Like a dog' is also the penultimate sentence of Kafka's *Trial*, and the phrase with which Sartre opens the same paragraph here, 'Vermine stupéfaite', now begins to look like another Kafka allusion, Gregor Samsa transformed overnight into a gigantic insect in *Metamorphosis*. Again, when Poulou finally mixes with his peer-group, 'Homme parmi les hommes' (p.187), this recalls the second sentence of another Kafka work, *Investigations of a Dog*: 'a dog among dogs'.

At this level, allusion is merging with parody and pastiche. Critics have recently been going through Sartre's fictions with a toothcomb to identify parodic elements, present to a truly remarkable degree, and the same is true of *Les Mots*. Philosophy as well as literature may supply the source-material. Geneviève Idt sees for instance in the numerous references to 'langage enfantin' — 'babillage', 'gribouillage', etc. — a deliberate parodic use of Heidegger's notion of 'bavardage' (a perhaps tendentious translation of the concept of *Gerede*), and

behind the motif of Everyman, a further Heideggerian allusion
to 'das Man' (*20*, pp.68-69). In this way, she detects behind the
whole book a 'polémique cachée' with Heidegger, usually
regarded as the most powerful influence on Sartre's thought
(and thus one to whom he prefers to hide his debt behind such
parodic treatment?). It seems to me she may well be right,
although as I have shown I think there is much more to the
notion of Sartre as Everyman. But how many readers can be
expected to follow the more esoteric allusions, and what have
they lost if they cannot? Parody is a kind of game, cultural
name-dropping, and it is possible that Sartre, attempting to put
himself in a position of superiority, is simply being clever at the
reader's expense. In parody there must always be an implied if
uneasy compliment, since there is no point in parodying
unknown or mediocre work. So perhaps the technique backfires,
as the parodist proves derivative, standing on the shoulders of
his model.

At any rate, spotting the allusions is a game sophisticated
readers can attempt to play; and no doubt Sartre himself took
pleasure in inserting them. Sometimes, as in the case of the
Kafka parody above, they are doubled up. Another example is
the Proustian allusion to Marcel's first visit to the theatre
(p.102), which is followed, three pages later, still in the context
of the early cinema, by a further reference, to involuntary
memory, at a deliberately 'unpoetic' level: 'quand je respire,
dans les cabinets d'un hôtel provincial, une certaine odeur de
désinfectant, quand, dans un train de nuit, je regarde au plafond
la veilleuse violette, je retrouve dans mes yeux, dans mes
narines, sur ma langue les lumières et les parfums de ces salles
disparues' (pp.105-06). Flaubert, a major preoccupation of
Sartre's at the time, is a frequent target. Gide, too, is cut down
to size, not only by being bracketed with Fantômas, but by the
mocking phrase, 'l'écœurante fadeur de ma disponibilité'
(p.146). Jules Romains comes in for similar treatment: we read
of 'une petite foule unanime' (p.187), but in the demeaning
context of Poulou's childish games. The vocabulary of Malraux
points to another butt: 'arracher ma vie au hasard' (p.210). And
so on.

The allusive technique has one further advantage: it enables Sartre to avoid, usually, the rebarbative jargon of complicated coinings and hyphenated constructions (a further, unfortunate legacy from Heidegger), which characterize, and to some minds disfigure, his works. Not always: describing Poulou's early fictional strivings, the term 'distanciation' and 'radicaliser' trip on to his pen (p.125). But these are rare lapses, and it is difficult to avoid the conclusion that complex notions were well within Sartre's expressive capabilities without his needing to employ abstract terminology. This, in his philosophical works, may indeed serve to obscure the psychological origins of much apparent 'metaphysical' thought. In *Les Mots* these roots are made clear.

One curious feature of *Les Mots* is that comments, on the surface directed against others, can be applied just as aptly to Sartre himself. We have seen this in the case of Louise, 'la négation pure' (p.13); on the same page, we read: 'Naturalistes et puritains — cette combinaison de vertus est moins rare qu'on ne pense — les Schweitzer aimaient les mots crus qui, tout en rabaissant très chrétiennement le corps, manifestaient leur large consentement aux fonctions naturelles'. This mixture of sexual crudity in expression and distaste for the flesh is a trait which struck readers of Sartre's early fiction, the first sparking off attacks against him for obscenity, though in today's climate it might well pass unnoticed. Both have generally been taken as evidence of Sartre's own psychological make-up. Or again, discussing Karl's attitude to money — 'Mon grand-père n'avait jamais su compter: prodigue par insouciance, généreux par ostentation' (p.39) — we recognize something very close to Sartre's own behaviour, mulled over at length in late-life interviews.

This feature may be another aspect of Sartre's narcissism; but inevitably the effect, intended or not, is to increase the impression of hereditary psychological elements. The device is even taken to the point of satirizing his own attitudes, such as the Everyman stance. Karl is made to quote Terence: '"Je suis homme, répétait-il d'une voix publique, je suis homme et rien d'humain ne m'est étranger"' (p.51); the 'cabotinage' is underlined by the 'voix publique'. Examples could be multiplied. Satire in others of traits Sartre knew he too possessed may have seemed more palatable than direct portrayal of them in himself.

At other times, though, Sartre uses self-disparagement as ego-defence. Thus he ironizes on his physique, his lack of stature and 'laideur'. Curiously, he even compares himself to Marshal Pétain: 'j'offris ma personne à la France' (p.96). Or again, on his late start as a published writer: 'Aux environs de 1930 les gens commenceraient à s'impatienter, ils se diraient entre eux: "Il prend son temps, celui-là! Voici vingt-cinq ans qu'on le nourrit à ne rien faire!"' (p.144). Here he is exorcizing the demon of anxiety, his very real fear of failure in the 1930s, connected with periods of depression during the Le Havre years. Perhaps the best example of this type of defensive irony occurs when he parries criticisms of his style by appearing to admit their justice: 'Il est vrai que je ne suis pas doué pour écrire; on me l'a fait savoir, on m'a traité de fort en thème: j'en suis un; mes livres sentent la sueur et la peine, j'admets qu'ils puent au nez de nos aristocrates' (p.139). Of course he is not really admitting this, but warding it off with false modesty and once more identifying himself with the ordinary man against the 'aristocrates'. This particular criticism, not unfair when applied to others of Sartre's works, provides an additional reason why *Les Mots* is deliberately one of the most sustained pieces of sparkling writing in the whole of French literature.

Of course most of us would prefer, if criticism of us has to be made, to make it ourselves, and Sartre is no exception: 'pour l'autocritique, je suis doué, à la condition qu'on ne prétende pas me l'imposer' (p.201). As Dr Johnson put it, shrewd as always: 'All censure of a man's self is oblique praise. It is in order to show how much he can spare'. And what really emerges from a consideration of the dozens of literary allusions, overt, concealed, or parodic, in Sartre's work (not only *Les Mots*), is to what degree he is steeped in literary tradition, as much as any writer of the century. His published criticism is far from generous, and *Qu'est-ce que la littérature?* is, among other things, a swingeing indictment of whole generations of novelists, not only of the past, but of the inter-war period, his own apprentice years. But this negative stance, claiming to reject traditional aesthetic values, has been a feature of the Artist since the Romantics, itself a tradition. In Sartre's recently published *Carnets* and correspondence, though, wider literary sympathies are evident, and influences not previously obvious: Laforgue, Barrès, Larbaud, Montherlant, and Saint-Exupéry, while Duhamel's *La Possession du monde* (1919), we can now see as crucial in Sartre's belief in knowledge by intuition, just as his *Scènes de la vie future* (1930) was to a whole generation of French anti-Americanism, including Sartre's own. There is even something of magpie eclecticism in this use of other writers and their ideas: Maurice Merleau-Ponty claimed about 1945 that he no longer discussed his ideas with Sartre, such was the danger they might be borrowed and not returned.

So it is not surprising, and certainly not through misinterpretation, that critics have so easily been able to 'recuperate' Sartre and *Les Mots* into the mainstream mandarin tradition of French literature he so affects to despise. It is where he belongs, despite the 'adieu' and the resolute forward-looking posture. Even the Romantic notion of posthumous *gloire*, indeed, can be placed in this further perspective, with Du Bellay: 'Heureux de qui la mort de sa gloire est suivie'.

It is thus fully appropriate that the internal ambivalence of *Les Mots* should be reflected in its external reception. The greatest irony is of course that of a work at least purporting to climax in a scornful farewell to literature should have received the accolade of the Nobel Prize for Literature — which he equally scornfully rejected: another example of 'cabotinage'? At least Rimbaud, whose gesture may have been in Sartre's mind, did abandon literature shortly if not immediately after *Une Saison en enfer*.

Irony extends to the very title of the book, woodenly translated as *The Words* in the American (but not English) edition. The definite article, detrimental as well as superfluous, deprives the reader not only of the Shakespearean allusion, 'Words, words, words', but also of the opposition with the missing term, 'things', several times stressed in the text. Words indeed, not things, not facts, much less human beings, were what primarily mattered to Sartre throughout his career: 'je crus avoir ancré mes rêves dans le monde par les grattements d'un bec d'acier' (p.121).

One of the most poignant moments in the book could scarcely have been intended by its author: the memory of Poulou, reproached by his mother with scribbling in inadequate light, replying, 'Même dans le noir je pourrais écrire'. Then comes the vision: 'sur la fin de ma vie, plus aveugle encore que Beethoven ne fût [*sic*] sourd, je confectionnerais à tâtons mon dernier ouvrage' (p.173). The irony is here involuntary, since a decade after the publication of *Les Mots* the affliction which struck down Sartre was, precisely, blindness; but it is none the less cruel. He was indeed to spend the last six years of his life in darkness, and the irony is compounded by the sad fact that he could *not* write in such conditions. His career as a writer was over. This is perhaps the clearest case ever of the *hubris* of a writer predicting, even in jest, his own future, a true irony of fate.

One of the most striking consequences of the book is another incidental irony: that, if we are to take Sartre seriously, it completely undermines, as we have seen, — or 'deconstructs' — the notion of Existential choice, since the whole thrust of the book is that the thirty years of 'folie', the Sartre he became and now rejects, were simply the product of his family and milieu, portrayed with retrospective loathing, resentment, and blame. Away from the dazzle of the rhetoric, there is something truly absurd about the apostle of free will and responsibility claiming that until his forties he was the unwitting and unwilling passive victim of his early childhood. The conventional view is that although adults are by definition responsible for their own beliefs, everyone is thus marked, to some extent; what is extra-ordinary is that Sartre tried to deny it for so long: 'Des amis s'étonnaient, quand j'avais trente ans: "On dirait que vous n'avez pas eu de parents. Ni d'enfance." Et j'avais la sottise d'être flatté' (p.200). Now their spectre is back with a vengeance, and Sartre's Existentialism is revealed as very much an attempt to deny determinism simply by turning his back on it and loudly affirming, without much effort to counter hostile arguments, the supremacy of individual will and choice in a grandiose rejection of any kind of dependence on others.

In any case, there is something odd about great men who complain about their background, however painful or miserable it may have been, although in English letters it is almost traditional to lament the bullying and general philistinism of boarding school, usually contrasted with a pre-school domestic paradise. They should not forget that, if their early years had been different, they might well not have become the adult or enjoyed the successful career they did. Humiliation in particular seems to act as a puissant catalyst. Not only does Existential choice get short shrift. The Sartrean distinction between contingency and necessity we can also trace back to Poulou's fear of death, on the one hand, and his loneliness and isolation from other children, on the other. In the latter case, certainly, and probably also the former, the problem can be seen as less metaphysical than psychological, and thus reduced in significance to the level of an irrational childhood phobia, like fear of the dark. More fundamental ambivalence.

8. Conclusion

There is no easy way of summing up *Les Mots*. A many-faceted work, it can be read simultaneously on a number of different levels of meaning, or as a 'palimpsest', to use a critical metaphor recently popularized by Gérard Genette. As such, it can be appreciated by readers with brows both high and low. On the most simple plane, the book is a description and examination of what purports to be Sartre's childhood in terms of his vocation as a writer. At the same time it is a debunking repudiation of that same vocation and a settling of accounts with the hated bourgeoisie, 'la tentative de destruction d'un mythe', as Sartre himself maintained in his preface to the Russian translation. (*Les Mots* is apparently the only one of his books to have been accorded Russian translation, an ungracious reward for all his years of — intermittent — fellow-travelling, and no doubt the denunciation of bourgeois society was why translation of the book was permitted.)

Then *Les Mots* is a set-piece of rhetorical writing, a demonstration of Sartre's ability with the pen. His challenge to literature must be an undisputed literary masterpiece: even if he has lost interest in purely literary quality, as he claims, he can still produce it better than any rival. There may be an element of self-justification here. If *Les Mots* is perhaps the most brilliantly written book of the century, its immediate predecessor, the *Critique de la raison dialectique*, is certainly one of the clumsiest, and had attracted much hostile comment. But in any case the *mea culpa* rapidly transforms itself into apologia, the negative soul-searching into positive self-justification.

Thus behind this modest-looking volume lies a gigantic artistic ambition. Not for him Karl's Aurillac vision of 'la carrière appliquée d'un écrivain mineur' (p.138); he will write a book which will rival, even surpass, the classic autobiographies of Rousseau, Goethe, and Gide, in the canon of acknowledged masterpieces. He is determined to do something different from what autobiographies have done before him (Malraux's aim too, composing his *Antimémoires* a few years later), and he will do it better, precisely by employing all existing techniques and refining on them by placing himself in a position of superiority through the pervasive irony. In particular, twentieth-century autobiographies, which Sartre might otherwise feel breathing down his neck, can be put in their place. If Michel Leiris uses the thematic order of narrative in *L'Age d'homme*, then Sartre will excel him by doing the same thing under the guise of a conventional chronological account. Julien Benda, in his *L'Enfance d'un clerc* (a title which fits Sartre's own book), analyses in great detail the various strands of experience which made him the man he was to become; Sartre will show this ponderous pedant how to do the same thing in light allusive style. Jean Guéhenno, as a *normalien* closer to home, is simply shown the door through parody of the culminating passage of his *Journal d'un homme de 40 ans*.

The keynote here behind the sustained dazzle of the writing is that of the self-conscious author, who at all times knows full well what he is about and who remains absolutely in control of his narrative. He is not interested in resolving the traditional difficulties of autobiography, but rather in exploiting its subtle contradictions by taking them as far as he can and thus making his work the most problematic of all in this, the most equivocal of literary genres. 'Ce que je viens d'écrire est faux. Vrai. Ni vrai ni faux' (p.61). This term, 'problematic', over-used in recent criticism, is here entirely apposite. Everything in the book gives rise to problems and paradox; nothing is as simple as it seems, from the text itself to Sartre's motives for writing it, an almost inextricable web as he uses, by parody and therefore contestation, the various myths and conventions of the genre. And Poulou, therefore Sartre himself, is an obvious descendant of the traditional Romantic 'problematic hero', introspective, self-questioning and timorous, compensating through fantasies an inability to take decisive action in real life. There is thus much more to his development than the psychodramas of the spoiled only child, living a hothouse existence cooped up in the Rue Le

Goff flat. It was, after all, the Romantic obsession with self and subjectivity which made the genre of autobiography leap in popularity in the nineteenth century.

In the end, the reader is entitled to doubt how far *Les Mots* is truly watertight and impervious to external criticism. At first reading one is swept along by the rhetoric. On reflection, one may well wonder, not so much if Sartre's memories are authentic as whether the whole drift of the argument is on the rational plane at all. Paradox and ambivalence — which can be redefined as self-contradiction — pervade every page. But ambivalence may be deliberate and systematic just as well as subconscious and revelatory, and one cannot be certain that Sartre, far from involuntarily revealing a 'sous-texte', has not been consciously mystifying his readers in a supreme exercise in 'cabotinage'. Thus Freudians have had a field-day with Poulou's relationship with his mother — 'plus tard je l'épouserai pour la protéger' (p.21) — forgetting that such comments may have been included precisely for their delectation. This is quite apart from the major vice in psychoanalytic method: if it suits, take what Sartre says literally, if it does not, make it mean its opposite by judicious interpretation of symbols.

This 'ludic' quality works both ways. If Sartre can evade criticism by claiming, of course I'm not really serious, then the reader can turn the ambivalence back on him, retorting, ah, but you're not really joking, either. Humiliations like the revelation of Poulou's 'laideur' were, despite disclaimers, never successfully exorcized. Perhaps it was even half his intention to immortalize them in the autobiography, like flies in amber. If narcissism implies self-hatred as well as self-love, it must involve assuming negative as much as positive aspects of personality and experience: warts and all. As Sartre himself wrote, in his preface to André Gorz's *Le Traître* (1958), nominally writing about Gorz but very probably with himself also in mind: 'derrière ces fulgurations se cache un enfant défunt qui se préfère à tout.'[14] And Sartre only achieves his masterpiece of irony at the cost of exploding the intellectual basis of his main philosophical

[14] Reprinted in *Situations*, IV, Gallimard, 1964, p.40,

concepts. But in the end the reader, not the author, inevitably has the last word in interpretation and evaluation, and admiration of the writing does not entail acceptance of everything at face value.

My own interpretation is that Sartre's attempt at self-justification in *Les Mots* did not succeed in assuaging his retrospective guilt at refusing to assist the anti-Fascist struggle in the 1930s. After all, self-disculpation by wholesale blame of others is neither mature not admirable behaviour. The blurred final pages of the book surely indicate that, far from having finally resolved his problems, which went way beyond resentment of a childhood which he felt humiliated him in his adult *orgueil*, Sartre was far from happy with his own argument. The intolerance and violence of many of his political reactions — both before and after 1963 —, culminating in applauding the murder of the Israeli athletes at the 1972 Olympics, show a sadly disturbed personality, in which guilt and self-hatred were still casting round wildly for an external target. One does not need a Freudian analysis to come to this conclusion, simply to apply the test of consistency to all Sartre's writings in the light of the thesis of *Les Mots*.

So it is clear that 'realism' need have little to do with *Les Mots*; nor accurate presentation of self. It may be true we have a better picture of Sartre's real self in the fiction, or even in Simone de Beauvoir's *L'Invitée*. *Jean sans terre* must have been a fairly crude attempt to fit Sartre's development into an orthodox Marxist matrix of political conversion; and the thesis of the work now, the internalization of a 'névrose', if more subtle, is an equally artificial construct, an 'illusion rétrospective', to use Sartre's own term (p.168), thrust into a Procrustean bed of tardy enlightenment about the true nature of his literary vocation. In both cases, the 'project' is propagandist and polemical, rather than analytical and explicative. Both theses cannot be right, but they could both be wrong, Sartre simply replacing one myth by another, the caricature of bourgeois optimism or the systematic deformation of Sartre as Everyman.

Where, then, does *Les Mots* stand as a work of literature? Philippe Lejeune has suggested (5, p.243) that, for posterity,

Sartre may be remembered primarily for *Les Mots*, just as for today's general reader Rousseau is above all the author of the *Confessions* (and Voltaire of *Candide*, one might add). But if so, it may be on a different level from conventional auto-biography. Another perceptive critic, Jacques Brenner, has commented that here 'Sartre nous donne *L'Enfance d'un écrivain* comme il nous avait donné autrefois *L'Enfance d'un chef*. Ce sont deux récits imaginaires'.[15] This brings us back to the idea that *Les Mots* cannot be bracketed off from Sartre's fiction, or from his biographical studies. In all three, his way of writing — as indeed in all his books — is assertive and imaginative, an essentially fictional mode. In this perspective, contradictions do not really matter, because his primary commitment is not to historical accuracy but to the illusion he creates. His raw material is drawn very much from his own narcissistic preoccupations, and critics have been able to demon-strate convincing parallels between, especially, the boy Lucien in *L'Enfance d'un chef*, Poulou, and their respective mothers. In fiction, indeed, psychological inconsistency may be taken simply as evidence of the hero's perplexity as to the meaning of his life.

This brings us back to the notion of the distinction between autobiography and fiction. As Georges May has sensibly noted, in both genres 'l'écrivain travaille avec sa mémoire et avec son imagination: seul varie d'un bout à l'autre de l'éventail le rôle relatif de ces deux facultés'. In this spectrum the autobio-graphical novel, especially narrated in the first person, merges into imaginative autobiography. Firm classification thus may become arbitrary: 'le roman et l'autobiographie sont les deux formes extrêmes que peut prendre un vaste genre littéraire qui se propose d'une manière générale de faire un livre d'une vie humaine'. It is thus not surprising autobiography uses narrative techniques already brought to maturity in the novel, since the latter's popularity as a genre came to maturity in the eighteenth century, long preceding that of autobiography. This is still true, and May observes that what Sartre wrote in 1948, in his preface to Nathalie Sarraute's *Portrait d'un inconnu*, fits *Les Mots*

---

[15] J. Brenner, *Histoire de la littérature française de 1940 à aujourd'hui*, Fayard, 1978, p.216.

equally if for the word 'roman' we substitute 'autobiographie': 'il s'agit de contester le roman par lui-même, de le détruire sous nos yeux dans le temps qu'on semble l'édifier'.[16]

And of course we need not look in autobiography any more than fiction for eternal psychological or philosophical truths; both genres can apprehend the universal only insofar as it is embodied in the particular. But any satisfactory autobiography will be a social and human document; Sartre adds to this aesthetic and intellectual preoccupations.

So if on one plane *Les Mots* can be read purely as a kind of negative *Bildungsroman*, to narrow the scope of the work in this way is to make it just as tendentious as the late nineteenth-century thesis novels so despised by Sartre. In my view there is much more to the book than this. Like all Sartre's best works, it is provocative, irritating, and fascinating at the same time, as indeed he intended: 'je voulais que ce soit agaçant, ce livre.'[17] As such its brilliance and verve are its own justification, while it contains the tantalizing mixture of the familiar and the unexpected which seems essential in great books.

I should like to end on a slightly different note. Unfair, even perverse, though it may be, *Les Mots* is very funny. Attempts to explicate humour are inevitably leaden-footed, since it can be best appreciated only by direct contact, so I have not dwelt on this aspect, although it obviously explains the work's popular appeal. Suffice it to say that reading selected passages in class can reduce hardbitten final-year literature students to helpless laughter. What better tribute could there be?

---

[16] May, op.cit., pp.187, 194-95, 172.

[17] *Sartre: un film réalisé par Alexandre Astruc et Michel Contat*, Gallimard, 1977, p.112.

Select Bibliography

indicates especially useful works.

A. CRITICAL EDITION OF 'LES MOTS'

*1. Ed. D. Nott (London, Methuen, 1981).

B. BOOKS ON 'LES MOTS'

2. A.J. Arnold & J.-P. Piriou, *Genèse et critique d'une autobiographie: 'Les Mots' de Jean-Paul Sartre* (Paris, Minard, 1973).
*3. E. Morot-Sir, *'Les Mots' de Jean-Paul Sartre* (Paris, Hachette, 1975).

C. BOOKS CONTAINING A SECTION ON 'LES MOTS'

4. D. LaCapra, *A Preface to Sartre* (London, Methuen, 1979).
*5. P. Lejeune, *Le Pacte autobiographique* (Paris, Seuil, 1975).
6. J. Mehlman, *A Structural Study of Autobiography: Proust, Leiris, Sartre, Lévi-Strauss* (Cornell University Press, 1974).
*7. J. Pacaly, *Sartre au miroir: une lecture psychanalytique de ses écrits biographiques* (Paris, Klincksieck, 1980).
8. J. Pilling, *Autobiography and Imagination: studies in self-scrutiny* (London, Routledge, 1981).
9. M. Scriven, *Sartre's Existential Biographies* (London, Macmillan, 1984).
10. P. Sénart, *Chemins critiques* (Paris, Plon, 1966).
11. P.-H. Simon, *Diagnostic des lettres françaises contemporaines* (Brussels, La Renaissance du Livre), 1966.
*12. P. Thody, *Sartre: a biographical introduction* (London, Studio Vista), 1971.

ARTICLES ON 'LES MOTS'

13. J. Behar, 'Jean-Paul Sartre: the great awakening', *Centennial Review*, XIV (1967), pp.549-64.
*14. M. Bensimon, 'D'un mythe à l'autre: essai sur les *Mots* de J.-P. Sartre', *Revue des Sciences Humaines*, XXX (1965), pp.415-30.
15. D. Boak, 'The genesis of *Les Mots*', *Essays in French Literature*, 21 (1984), pp.81-88.
*16. V. Brombert, 'Sartre et la biographie impossible', *Cahiers de l'Association Internationale des Etudes Françaises*, VII (1967), pp.155-66.

17. H.F. Ellenberger, 'Les Mots de Sartre', Dialogue: Canadian Philosophical Review, III (1965), pp.433-37.

18. J.P. Fell, 'Sartre's Words: an existential self-analysis', Psychoanalytical Review, LV (1968), pp.426-41.

19. R. Girard, 'L'Anti-héros et les salauds', Mercure de France, 353 (1965), pp.422-49.

*20. G. Idt, 'L'Autoparodie dans Les Mots de Sartre', Cahiers du 20ᵉ Siècle, 6 (1976), pp.53-86.

*21. ——, 'Modèles scolaires dans l'écriture sartrienne', Revue des Sciences Humaines, 174 (1979), pp.83-103.

*22. ——, 'Des Mots á L'Enfance d'un chef: autobiographie et psychanalyse', in M. Issacharoff & J.-C. Vilquin ed., Sartre et la mise en signe (Paris, Klincksieck, 1982), pp.11-30.

23. S.-C. Josa, 'Les Mots: vivre dans la contingence', Esprit, 32 (1964), pp.654-59.

24. R. Kanters, 'Moi, dis-je, et c'est assez', Revue de Paris, 71 (Feb. 1964), pp.115-23.

*25. J. Lecarme, 'Les Mots de Sartre: un cas limite de l'autobiographie?', Revue d'Histoire Littéraire de la France, LXXV (1975), pp.1047-66.

26. A. Patri, 'Sartre avant les maux', Preuves, 14 (May 1964), pp.72-77.

27. R.P. Prentice, 'On Sartre's Les Mots', Antonianum, XLV (1970), pp.474-504.

*28. P. Thody, Sartre's Les Mots: a defence of normality', in B. Curtis & W. Mays ed., Phenomenology and Education (London, Methuen, 1978), pp.104-18.

29. J.P. Tompkins, 'Sartre Resartus: a reading of Les Mots', Romanic Review, 71 (1980), pp.47-56.

30. E.N. Zimmermann, 'Jean-Paul Sartre's Les Mots: problems in criticism', Criticism, VI (1964), pp.313-23.

CRITICAL GUIDES TO FRENCH TEXTS

edited by
Roger Little, Wolfgang van Emden, David Williams